THE
EVANGELICAL
PRESIDENT

THE EVANGELICAL PRESIDENT

GEORGE BUSH'S STRUGGLE TO
SPREAD A MORAL DEMOCRACY
THROUGHOUT THE WORLD

❖

BILL SAMMON

Since 1947
REGNERY
PUBLISHING, INC.
An Eagle Publishing Company • Washington, DC

Library of Congress Cataloging-in-Publication Data

Sammon, Bill.
  The evangelical president / Bill Sammon.
      p. cm.
  Includes index.
  ISBN 978-1-59698-518-6
  1. Bush, George W. (George Walker), 1946- Political and social views.
  2. Bush, George W. (George Walker), 1946- Religion. 3. Evangelicalism-
Political aspects-United States. 4. Fundamentalism-Political aspects-United
States. 5. Christianity and politics-United States. 6. United States-Politics
and government-2001- 7. United States-Foreign relations-2001- 8. Cheney,
Richard B. 9. Iraq War, 2003- 10. War on Terrorism, 2001- I. Title.
  E903.3.S355 2007
  973.931092-dc22

                                                            2007030824

Published in the United States by

Regnery Publishing, Inc.
One Massachusetts Avenue, NW
Washington, DC 20001

www.regnery.com

Manufactured in the United States of America

10 9 8 7 6 5 4 3 2 1

To Billy

—❧·❦—

"We go forward with trust that the Author of Liberty will guide us through these trying hours."

GEORGE W. BUSH
Address to the Nation
January 10, 2007

Contents

Prologue
Bill Maher's Piñata 1

Chapter One
"My Faith Has Grown" 13

Chapter Two
"The Watershed Year" 33

Chapter Three
"A Case of Some of His Juniors Overreacting" 51

Chapter Four
"Don't Be a Jerk" 63

Chapter Five
The Decider 89

Chapter Six
Golf Cart One 101

Chapter Seven
Botched Jokes 115

Chapter Eight
"Bush Makes Me Sick" 139

Chapter Nine
"Can't Win 'Em All" 153

Chapter Ten
"The Author of Liberty" 163

Chapter Eleven
"The Creator of Life" 173

Chapter Twelve
"This War Is Lost" 185

Chapter Thirteen
Perspicacious 197

Acknowledgments 219
Index 221

Bill Maher's Piñata

"Do you think Bush prays a lot about Iraq?"

Coming from anyone else, the question would have been perfectly legitimate. But coming from comedian Bill Maher, whose contempt for President Bush was matched only by his contempt for religion, the question could be just one thing: a set-up for a partisan punch line.

Nonetheless, as the designated piñata on a panel of Bush-bashers, I had little choice but to attempt a straightforward answer.

"I think he prays a lot, period," I said, prompting derisive laughter from the Hollywood audience attending this taping of Maher's HBO show, *Real Time*. "He's an unapologetically religious person."

"I'm just asking because there was a story in the news last week that said they did a nine-year study," Maher said with practiced comic timing, "and prayer doesn't work."

The left-wing audience erupted in laughter and applause at this trashing of a practice held sacred by billions. I gritted my teeth and plowed ahead with an anecdote aimed at answering Maher's question.

"I was interviewing the president about when he pulled the trigger on Operation Iraqi Freedom," I said. "He had the war council over to the White House. He talked to the generals and Rumsfeld and so forth. He gave the decision to start the war. They left; he was alone in the Oval Office."

At this point I recounted my specific exchange with the president:

"What did you do next?" I asked the president.

"I went out to the South Lawn and walked around the running track a couple of times," Bush replied, noting that he was accompanied by only his dogs.

"Why?" I asked. "You just gave the order to go to war, and now you're out walking around the South Lawn? What were you doing?"

"I was praying," Bush said.

A lone member of Maher's audience guffawed loudly. I ignored him and continued recounting the president's explanation.

"I had just made the most momentous decision a president could make—sending young men and women into harm's way—and I needed God's guidance," Bush said.

A lone member of Maher's audience guffawed loudly. I ignored him and continued recounting the president's explanation.

Turning to Maher, I concluded: "That's the kind of thing that conservatives like about Bush."

"It is," Maher agreed.

"Liberals?" I added. "It makes them crazy."

Ignoring this barb, Maher continued trolling for yuks by further denigrating Bush's belief in God.

"I constantly read things in the news about how the president or someone high up in his administration didn't know something really kind of crucial about Iraq—like that there are Sunnis and Shiites," Maher deadpanned, sparking laughter.

"And my guess is that he was praying when he should have been learning," he added to the sound of cheers and applause. "And I don't say that, you know, as a snarky remark. I really mean it."

Bill Maher claiming not to be snarky would be like Senator Joe Biden claiming not to be bombastic. The Delaware Democrat, who was also a guest on the show, now took his turn at impugning the president's religious authenticity.

"Smart people pray. This guy uses it in a way, I think, to avoid having to know the hard things," Biden said as the audience tried to gauge whether he was serious. "No, I mean it."

"Yes," Maher said, "you're right."

"Republicans seem to use prayer as a political, organizational tool, not a road to redemption," Biden said, earning applause. "But I respect the fact that the president prays. That is totally separable from the fact whether or not the president is informed."

Biden, who was in the early stages of mounting a long-shot bid to succeed Bush, was not content to deride the president as both uninformed and cynical. The senator also felt compelled to portray himself as having gotten the better of Bush in private conversations.

"When I speak to the president—and I have had plenty of opportunity to be with the president, at least prior to the last election, a lot of hours alone with him. I mean, meaning me and his staff," said Biden, amending his boast. "And the president will say things to me, and I'll literally turn to the president, say, 'Mr. President, how can you say that, knowing you don't know the facts?' And he'll look at me and he'll say—my word—he'll look at me and he'll say, 'My instincts.' He said, 'I have good instincts.' I said, 'Mr. President, your instincts aren't good enough.'"

The audience was eating up this dubious account of Bush getting his comeuppance from the intrepid senator. Suitably encouraged, Biden warned against the prospect of Bush conflating "prayer with guidance in where to send your missiles." "If he does that, then that's dangerous, that's over the edge," Biden said. "I don't think that's what he does. I think he makes these decisions based on his instincts and then prays he's right."

Cheers, laughter, applause all around.

"I have my own faith," allowed Biden, a Catholic. "The problem with a lot of elites in the Democratic Party, quite frankly, is they communicate they don't respect people's faith."

To illustrate his point, Biden launched into a rambling anecdote that, if nothing else, shed some light on whether he possessed the temperament to have his finger on the nuclear button. "I'll give you a very quick story," he falsely promised. "My mother, God love her, very smart woman. Eighty-nine years old. Lives with me. Good health. My mother says a rosary every Sunday at Mass—when we go to Mass—for her deceased brother Ambrose, who died in New Guinea, and the body was never recovered. I said to one of my colleagues—who is a very sophisticated guy—when we got in an argument, I said, 'Okay, Charlie, this is what my mother does. What do you think of that?' And he looked at me and said, 'I think that's *quaint*.' And I said, 'Were we not senators, I'd rip your goddamn Adam's apple out, because who the hell are you to look at my mother and say it's "*quaint*"?' We have too many elites in our party who look down their nose on people of faith," Biden concluded. "The people of faith don't want us to share their view. They just want to know we respect them. We *respect* them. That's the big problem with my party."

Actually, "the people of faith" would be delighted if more politicians shared their view. And in the unlikely event that any of them were watching *Real Time*, they would have been appalled by how patronizing Biden sounded. By insisting that Democrats make a show of "respecting" religious Americans whose beliefs their party rejected, Biden was himself looking down his nose at evangelical Christians, including Bush. The condescending senator might as well have called religious Americans "quaint."

Not to be outdone, fellow Democratic panelist Ben Affleck, an actor in the midst of a box-office slump (thanks to flops such as *Gigli*), felt compelled to establish his own religious bona fides.

"I'm a Christian," he blurted. "I have prayed in my life." It came out almost as an apology, the way Jimmy Carter once admitted, "I've committed adultery in my heart." Sensing he may have gone too far for the relentlessly secular Maher, Affleck backpedaled by assuring the audience that he was no more than "a vaguely religious person" with a "basic sense of moral center." Or at least that's what "people want to think" about him, the actor surmised.

Affleck then assailed Bush for wearing his religion on his sleeve. "It's because he doesn't have anything else to tout," he railed. "And touting religion—absent any thought—is a terrible mistake, and really, you know, almost criminal. I mean, the history of the world is filled with religious people who were really smart, like, you know, Shakespeare and Alexander Pope and Newton. I mean, science was developed by people of great faith. They're not mutually exclusive."

Wow.

To bring some "balance" to this learned debate, Maher then turned to author Kevin Phillips, a media darling because he had renounced the GOP decades earlier after working for President Nixon. The Left still disingenuously referred to him as a Republican, because the label gave Phillips a certain media cachet reserved for those who trash their own party. To that end, Phillips had just published a book titled *American Theocracy*, in which he argued that America was being destroyed by Christian fundamentalism. It never seemed to occur to such leftists that Islamic fundamentalism might be a bigger threat to America than Christian fundamentalism.

"Religiosity and support for the Republican Party have sort of become synonymous," Phillips told Maher. "I think that's a problem, because it then produces within the Republican Party an attempt to get politics and religion closer and closer, and verges on some very dangerous ideas."

Maher pointed out that a woman in Cleveland had asked Bush about *American Theocracy* a few weeks earlier.

"Former Nixon administration official Kevin Phillips," the woman began, blithely perpetuating the fiction that Phillips was a Republican, "discusses what has been called radical Christianity and its growing involvement into government and politics. He makes the point that members of your administration have reached out to prophetic Christians who see the war in Iraq and the rise of terrorism as signs of the apocalypse. Do you believe this, that the war in Iraq and the rise of terrorism are signs of the apocalypse? And if not, why not?"

The audience at the City Club of Cleveland openly howled at the question, but Bush remained gracious.

"I haven't really thought of it that way," he demurred with a smile. "First I've heard of that, by the way. I guess I'm more of a practical fellow."

Clearly, Bush did not buy into the book's thesis. But that didn't stop Maher from trying to portray the president as a dangerous zealot.

"I think he kind of avoided the question," the host complained to Phillips. "But he is an end-timer, is he not? He is someone, like many evangelicals, who believes that the end of our days are near. And doesn't this affect someone's policy, their thinking on matters that affect the rest of us—who don't think end times are near?"

The audience, through its laughter, left no doubt whose side it was on.

"That's exactly right," Phillips said. "I can't tell you that I know that George W. thinks the end times are coming, but 45 percent of American Christians, according to *Newsweek*, believe in the end times and Armageddon. And within the evangelical, Pentecostal, and fundamentalist groups that support George W., it's a lot higher. So my guess is that probably about 55 percent of the people who voted for him believe in this. They think about the prophesies in the book of Revelation and they expect this to happen. And that's why I think he couldn't answer that question in Cleveland, simply because if he said he believed in the apocalypse and Armageddon and the end times, all of a sudden, something like 30 percent or 40 percent of his electorate would say, 'Oh, boy!' On the other hand, you know, a lot of people *believe*. And if he was in any way critical of it—and I think even evading it made them nervous—then maybe he really doesn't fully believe in the Bible."

In other words, when it came to the notion of end times, Bush was either a kook for believing it or an apostate for doubting it. As usual, it was impossible for the president to take a position that could satisfy the Left.

Phillips went on to argue that Bush's supposed religiosity would cause nothing less than the ruination of the United States. He claimed this was clear from the history of other great nations that fell. "In their later stages of power, they tend to think they have more power than they have. They often overreach. They often get carried away with a kind of evangelical religion, that they're out to spread morality around the world," he warned. "Obviously, what has gone wrong before is in the process of going very wrong again for the United States. And it's ironic that George W. majored in history at Yale, because I think he doesn't know any more about history than he knows about, you know, how to make fried calamari."

"Well spoken!" proclaimed Maher amid raucous applause and laughter. Then he turned to his designated piñata to try out another rehearsed joke.

"Let me ask you one more, and then we'll get off religion," Maher assured me. "It was big news this week that the missing link between sea animals and land animals was found. And it just struck me as funny, because I know what bothers creationists so much is the idea that man developed from something that crawled out of the slime. Well, this thing they found is *exactly* something that crawls out of the slime. It's *exactly* a fish that crawled out of the slime. What do you think the president thinks about this? And why are they so insecure about us coming from the apes? We're clearly superior to them. Clearly."

Once again, I tried to ignore the ensuing laughter and give a straightforward answer that stuck to the facts, not opinion. "I think this will reignite the whole argument about whether intelligent design should be taught alongside evolution in our schools," I ventured. "And, as you know, President Bush came out some months ago and said that it should be. Very controversial. Some people think only evolution should be taught. And Bush believes that both should."

The notion that some people actually believed that man was created in the image of God and did not descend from a prehistoric fish was simply too much for Biden.

"This is reversible, man, this is *reversible*!" he exclaimed. "We don't have to go down this road! I refuse to believe the majority of people believe this malarkey!"

"I agree," said Maher.

"I absolutely refuse to believe it!" Biden ranted. "There are a lot of people that are frightened now. It's not coincidental that there's a rise in fundamentalism in the last thirty years across the board, in every confessional faith. It's because people are losing control of their lives. They're losing control! They don't think they can affect what happens to them. And the more frightened—about 10 percent of those folks—they turn to really fundamental answers. But that doesn't mean the government doesn't have a responsibility, and leaders have a responsibility, to explain a way through this, a way to get out of this. And when government plays into this notion that, 'Oh, woe is me, we're down the drain; this is the end, Armageddon is on the way,' you just fuel it. I mean, we're—we just have to fight this. I mean, this is not—I refuse to believe that that's what the majority of American people think!"

Rapturous Hollywood applause followed for the presidential candidate who had just dismissed the sacrosanct beliefs of millions of creationists as "malarkey." Biden was evidently oblivious to Gallup polls that showed more Americans believed in creationism than evolution.

"I think the senator is right about that, and I think it's supported by what the author said," Affleck chirped. "The vast majority of Americans are religious. But very few of them are sort of, like, you know, slightly lunatic, fundamentalist nut-balls who say, 'Well, no, they—you know, we have to have been—the Earth is six thousand years old, and there were no dinosaurs.'"

Without bothering to explain the bizarre suggestion that evangelical Christians were dinosaur-deniers, Affleck abruptly seized the opportunity to crack a joke he had been saving up. "What I can say to those people—from experience—about Armageddon," grinned the actor who had starred in a disaster film of the same name, "is that it's *not good*!"

The audience roared.

❧

When I told President Bush this book would be called *The Evangelical President*, he said, "Meaning what?" As we sat down in the Oval Office, I explained that the title actually had two meanings—one religious and one secular. The religious meaning was obvious in that Bush had long been considered an evangelical Christian. But he could also be described as evangelical in the non-religious sense, meaning he was passionate about advocating something—in this case, the liberation of Iraq and the broader war against terrorism.

"You are really a true believer," I posited. "Some presidents haven't had that kind of belief."

I pointed out that unlike his father, who had famously struggled with "the vision thing," the younger Bush possessed a vision that, for better or worse, was considered audacious.

"Well, presidents get defined by the circumstances in which they find themselves," Bush replied. "I had a different set of circumstances."

The evangelical president explained that the tragedy of September 11 forced him to confront conditions in the Middle East that could "cause nineteen kids to be so affected that they got airplanes and killed nearly three thousand citizens. The security of America is at stake, the long-term solution of which will be changing forms of government, giving people a chance to be free," he said. "I passionately believe that freedom and liberty are universal and can change the world."

This idealistic ambition to "change the world" made Bush somewhat impervious to his critics, who were becoming legion down the home stretch of his presidency. "I definitely believe one role of a leader is to set a vision to which we ought to head," he told me. "I've always thought that it's important, one, to define the ideal, and to lead toward that ideal, recognizing that sometimes it's not a straight path and there's difficulties along the way. But I don't see how you can ask a people to follow unless they know where they're headed."

This, then, is the story of a president who was evangelical about both faith and war. It is the fourth installment in a multi-volume series of books chronicling the historic Bush presidency. The first of those volumes, *Fighting Back*, examined how September 11 utterly transformed the presidency. The second, *Misunderestimated*, documented the toppling of Iraqi dictator Saddam Hussein. The third, *Strategery*, chronicled Bush's reelection and the difficult first year of his second term.

The Evangelical President picks up where *Strategery* left off, which is to say the end of 2005, when the attacks that had bombarded the Bush White House for five years finally started to do real damage. Bush belatedly realized the folly of ignoring Democratic attacks on him and his powerful consigliere, Vice President Dick Cheney. The two began to fight back, but the relentlessly negative mainstream media was already predicting doom for Republicans in the midterm elections. Worse yet, al Qaeda leader Abu Musab al-Zarqawi remained one step ahead of U.S. forces in Iraq as he plotted to unleash mayhem on an unimaginable scale.

In these days, Bush stumbled. The stumbles ranged from the dire—serious setbacks in Iraq and Democratic victories in Congress—to the ridiculous—Dick Cheney's hunting accident and George Allen's "macaca" scandal.

But all was not lost. At long last, Saddam was being tried for his crimes against humanity. And spectacularly successful elections in Iraq were giving rise to hope that stability for the war-torn nation might finally be at hand.

That hope, alas, would prove premature.

BILL SAMMON
August 2007

Chapter One

"My Faith Has Grown"

A White House staffer propped Miss Beazley on her haunches and wiggled a forepaw as if the Scottish terrier were waving good-bye to President Bush as he headed to church. It was a sunny, pleasant Sunday morning, and the church was only a block away—just across leafy Lafayette Park—but the Secret Service was not about to let the president and First Lady Laura Bush actually traverse those two hundred yards on foot. In the post–September 11 era, security considerations precluded the president from taking even a short stroll through the sun-drenched park across from his own front yard. So at 7:39 AM, after untold preparations by countless Secret Service agents, White House staffers, and sleepy-eyed journalists, a massive presidential motorcade was arrayed along the gracefully curved driveway of the South Lawn. The First Couple emerged from the South Portico, climbed into the presidential limousine, and began the absurdly short ride to St. John's Episcopal Church. The procession included a decoy limousine, ambulance, vans filled with staffers, vans filled with journalists, and an armada of menacing black SUVs bristling with enough sophisticated communications equipment, sunglasses-wearing Secret Service agents, and state-of-the-art weaponry to start a small war. Miss Beazley, the presidential puppy, could only watch from the South Lawn in wonder.

Exactly three minutes later, the motorcade arrived at St. John's, also known as the "Church of Presidents." Every chief executive since James Madison had attended services at this small, unassuming structure, partly because it was so conveniently located. Bush, dressed in beige, and the First Lady, in gray, emerged from the limousine and greeted the pastor, the Reverend Dr. Luis León, in front of the Doric columns beneath the church's high steeple. The Bushes entered the yellow stucco building and headed for pew fifty-four, the "President's Pew," which was always reserved for the commander in chief and contained an eighteenth-century prayer book autographed by many of Bush's predecessors. Members of the public were also in attendance, including a group of school children visiting from California, who had to pass through metal detectors for the privilege of worshipping with the president.

The main scripture reading, Acts 2:1–21, described how the Holy Spirit descended upon the apostles, fulfilling a promise made by Jesus before his crucifixion.

> When the day of Pentecost had come, they were all together in one place. And suddenly from heaven there came a sound like the rush of a violent wind, and it filled the entire house where they were sitting. Divided tongues, as of fire, appeared among them, and a tongue rested on each of them. All of them were filled with the Holy Spirit and began to speak in other languages, as the Spirit gave them ability.

As the Reverend León recounted, this allowed the apostles to be understood by everyone in the cosmopolitan city of Jerusalem, which included people from Mesopotamia, or modern-day Iraq, as well as a litany of far-flung kingdoms that corresponded to modern-day Iran, Saudi Arabia, Egypt, Turkey, Rome, and Greece. As the astonished people of Jerusalem tried to make sense of this miracle, Peter reminded them God had vividly foretold the "last days" through the prophet Joel:

> I will show portents in the heaven above and signs on the earth below, blood, and fire, and smoky mist. The sun shall be turned to darkness and the moon to blood, before the coming of the Lord's great and glorious day. Then everyone who calls on the name of the Lord shall be saved.

If Kevin Phillips and Bill Maher had been in St. John's Episcopal, the former might have looked at the latter and said, "I told you so." But listening to an apocalyptic scripture reading did not make Bush an end-timer any more than worshipping in an Episcopal church made him an Episcopalian. Strictly speaking, Bush was a Methodist, having joined his wife's church back in 1982 after their twin daughters were baptized. Prior to that, he spent the first thirty-six years of his life switching back and forth between the churches of his mother, Presbyterian, and father, Episcopal.

"I was taught religion early," Bush told me in the Oval Office. "The seed had been planted by dutiful parents."

That seed began to sprout in 1959, when thirteen-year-old George and his family moved from West Texas to East Texas.

"My family had attended the First Presbyterian Church in Midland; with the move to Houston we began attending the Episcopal church, the denomination my dad was raised in," Bush explained in his 1999 memoir, *A Charge to Keep*. "I served communion at the 8 AM service at St. Martin's. I loved the formality, the ritual, the candles, and there I felt the first stirrings of a faith that would be years in the shaping."

That faith would be further shaped in 1973, when Bush took a job working with poor black children in Houston's inner city. It was a major culture shock for a privileged white guy who had graduated from both Phillips Academy—the elite boarding school in Andover, Massachusetts—and Yale.

"My job gave me a glimpse of a world I had never seen," Bush wrote in *A Charge to Keep*. "It was tragic, heartbreaking, and uplifting, all at the same time. I saw a lot of poverty. I also saw a lot of bad choices: drugs, alcohol abuse, men who had fathered children and walked away, leaving single mothers struggling to raise children on their own. I saw children who could not read and were way behind in school. I also saw good and decent people working to try to help lift these kids out of their terrible circumstances."

Some of these sights were downright shocking to the Ivy Leaguer whose father was chairman of the Republican National Committee. One day, for example, while Bush was playing basketball with some kids, a pre-teen went up for a jump shot and dropped a handgun on the court. Another time, Bush accompanied a six- or seven-year-old named Jimmy to a slum where the boy lived.

"I'll never forget taking him home," wrote Bush, who likened Jimmy to a "little brother." "The screen door was ripped, the front porch was rotting, the room inside was smoky, and the music was blaring. I walked Jimmy to his door and the woman who answered it was clearly stoned. I don't know what she was taking, but she was not in touch with reality. Jimmy was happy to be home, but I was incredibly sad to leave him there."

Bush left the inner city job after less than a year to return to the Ivy League—he had been accepted at Harvard Business School. Fifteen years later, when he visited Houston to eulogize the man who had given him that job, Bush learned Jimmy had been shot and killed. It was a reminder of the urban despair that had shocked his sensibilities back in 1973. Bush would later say his experiences in Houston helped shape his "no child left behind" educational reforms as governor and president.

In 1975, after earning a master of business administration degree from Harvard, Bush returned to his beloved Midland, Texas, where he had spent the formative years of his childhood. Like his father before him, he started teaching Sunday school at First Presbyterian. His faith was steady, although Bush was by no means a devoutly religious man. For one thing, by his own admission, he drank too much. "When I was young and irresponsible, I sometimes behaved young and irresponsibly," he would later quip. Although he settled down somewhat after meeting and marrying Laura in 1977, he remained spiritually restless for years.

"That seed was dormant," Bush told me, recalling the religious belief instilled by his parents. "There are moments in my life when I rejected prayer and rejected the need to rely upon something greater than myself."

The big change in his faith began in 1985, when the Reverend Billy Graham visited the Bush family's seaside compound, known as Walker's Point, in Kennebunkport, Maine. The famed evangelist was asked by Bush's father one evening to answer questions from a large group of family members who had gathered for the weekend.

"He sat by the fire and talked," Bush said of Graham in *A Charge to Keep*. "And what he said sparked a change in my heart. I don't remember the exact words. It was more the power of his example. The Lord was so clearly reflected in his gentle and loving demeanor. The next day we walked and talked at Walker's Point, and I knew that I was in the presence of a great man. He was like a magnet; I felt drawn to seek something different. He didn't lecture or admonish; he shared warmth and concern. Billy Graham didn't make you feel guilty; he made you feel loved. Over the course of that weekend, Reverend Graham planted a mustard seed in my soul, a seed that grew over the next years. He led me to the path, and I began walking. And it was the beginning of a change in my life."

Bush insisted he had always been "a religious person," citing his regular church attendance, his teaching of Sunday school, even his years as an altar boy. "But that weekend my faith took on new meaning," he explained. "It was the beginning of a new walk where I would recommit my heart to Jesus Christ. I was humbled to learn that God sent His son to die for a sinner like me. I was comforted to know that through the son, I could find God's amazing grace, a grace that crosses every border, every barrier, and is open to everyone. Through the love of Christ's life, I could understand the life-changing powers of faith."

Upon his return to Midland, Bush decided to take a fresh look at scripture. He joined a men's Bible study group at the suggestion of his friend Don Evans. The book they studied first was the Acts of the Apostles, complete with the story of the Pentecost and the apocalyptic prophesy about the sun turning "to darkness and the moon to blood." Bush was rapt. "It was a way to help focus," he told me. "All of us find our comfort zone—our comfort in religion—in a variety of ways. There's not a single path."

Evans gave Bush a Bible divided into 365 passages so the entire book could be read in a year. "My interest in reading the Bible grew stronger and stronger, and the words became clearer and more meaningful," he marveled. "I gained confidence and understanding in my faith."

Scripture was now a fixture in Bush's life. But then, so was alcohol.

"I was drinking too much," he wrote in *A Charge to Keep*. "Drinking also magnified aspects of my personality that probably didn't need to be larger than they already were—made me more funny, more charming (I thought), more irrepressible. Also, according to my wife, somewhat boring and repetitive. What may have been funny in moderation was not so funny in exaggeration."

The issue came to a head in July 1986, when both Bush and Evans turned forty. They celebrated by getting together with their wives and a few friends at the luxurious Broadmoor resort in Colorado Springs. By the end of the evening, Bush was feeling no pain.

"I just drank too much and woke up with a hangover," he recalled. "I got out of bed and went for my usual run. For the past fourteen years, I had run at least three miles almost every day. This run was different. I felt worse than usual, and about halfway through, I decided I would drink no more."

Upon reflection, Bush said his decision to stop drinking could be traced to the encounter a year earlier with Billy Graham. The preacher had somehow appealed to the ascetic in Bush, who now felt empowered by the discipline it took to reject alcohol.

"I quit drinking because of faith," Bush told me. "I believe that."

This faith-based decision became a significant turning point in his life. "Inwardly, I felt different," Bush wrote. "I had more time to read. I had more energy. I became a better listener, and not such an incessant talker. Quitting drinking made me more focused and more disciplined. I now say it is one of the best things I have ever done."

The yearlong period that began with Bush's encounter with Billy Graham and ended with his forswearing of alcohol amounted to the conversion experience that is one of the defining characteristics of an evangelical Christian. Granted, Bush had always been affiliated with mainline Protestant denominations—Methodist, Presbyterian, Episcopal—and not evangelical Protestant denominations like the Southern Baptist Convention or the Assemblies of God. But his evangelicalism was defined less by his membership in any particular church than by his beliefs and behavior. Generally speaking, evangelical Christians placed great emphasis on the need for a conversion experience such as Bush's. They believed people could not be born into faith, but rather had to come to it through a conversion experience that culminated in a commitment to Jesus Christ. Perhaps it was no accident, then, that Bush said his favorite hymn was "Amazing Grace," a psalm of a self-described "wretch" who rejoiced, "I once was lost, but now am found."

Bush told me the seed that had long lain dormant within him now "began to grow." "It was a reinvigoration of a religious belief," he explained. "I've recognized that prayer is an important part of my life and that there is a God and that I can rely upon that God for comfort and strength."

Still, Bush shied away from labeling himself "born again" or even "evangelical" because he knew his political opponents would twist those words against him. He said such designations could "obscure what it means to be a religious person." "These labels are loaded with all kinds of meanings that tend to undermine the seriousness of one's personal faith and the discipline and work and time that goes into maintaining as close a relationship with the Lord as you can possibly attain," Bush told me. "The reason I say that is because in politics, people tend to say, 'Well, you know, he is getting instructions from above,' or 'He only makes his decisions based upon this, that or the other.'"

And yet Bush was unapologetic about his religious conviction, even after entering national politics, as evidenced by his remarks during a 1999 Republican presidential debate in Iowa.

"What political philosopher or thinker," a moderator asked, "do you most identify with and why?"

While the other candidates named people like Thomas Jefferson or Abraham Lincoln, Bush gave a decidedly different answer.

"Christ," he replied matter-of-factly, "because he changed my heart."

"I think that the viewer would like to know more on how he has changed your heart," the moderator said.

"Well, if they don't know it's going to be hard to explain," Bush replied. "When you turn your heart and your life over to Christ, when you accept Christ as a savior, it changes your heart, and changes your life. And that's what happened to me."

Although many Americans found the answer refreshing, the secular press was outraged and attacked Bush accordingly. It was the sort of hostile coverage of Bush's faith that would continue throughout his presidency. Liberal writers asserted that Bush suffered from an acute messiah complex. He had "grand delusions of having been hand-picked by Jesus to shepherd this nation," wailed Michelle Cottle in the *New Republic* magazine.

The crucible of September 11 crystallized the president's religious convictions. Three days after the terrorist attacks, in his most memorable speech, Bush spoke without embarrassment about the epic themes of good and evil, grief and righteousness, cruelty and compassion, with a moral clarity that would come to define his presidency.

"Our responsibility to history is already clear: to answer these attacks and rid the world of evil," Bush vowed at the National Cathedral in Washington. "Yet our wounds as a people are recent and unhealed, and lead us to pray. In many of our prayers this week, there is a searching, and an honesty."

The president tried to console the shell-shocked nation by reminding Americans that the Lord worked in mysterious ways. "God's signs are not always the ones we look for. We learn in tragedy that His purposes are not always our own.... Yet the prayers of private suffering, whether in our homes or in this great cathedral, are known and heard—and understood. There are prayers that help us last through the day, or endure the night. There are prayers of friends and strangers that give us strength for the journey. And there are prayers that yield our will to a will greater than our own. This world He created is of moral design. Grief and tragedy and hatred are only for a time. Goodness, remembrance, and love have no end. And the Lord of life holds all who die, and all who mourn."

Bush ended the speech by unashamedly leading the nation in prayer. "On this national day of prayer and remembrance, we ask almighty God to watch over our nation, and grant us patience and resolve in all that is to come. We pray that He will comfort and console those who now walk in sorrow. We thank Him for each life we now must mourn, and the promise of a life to come. As we have been assured, neither death nor life, nor angels nor principalities nor powers, nor things present nor things to come, nor height nor depth, can separate us from God's love. May He bless the souls of the departed. May He comfort our own. And may He always guide our country. God bless America."

Karl Rove, the president's closest political adviser, looked back on the terrorist attacks as one of the moments in Bush's life when his religious convictions were strengthened the most. "I've seen faith deepen in his life," Rove told me. "There's nothing like war to open up your eyes to the importance of faith."

Bush agreed. "My faith has grown," he told me. "When you put kids into combat, it requires a lot of prayerful moments. It is the prayer of protecting them, for starters, and comforting their families." He added, "Probably the most powerful events that affected my thinking and my religion are when I meet with families of the fallen. And it's remarkable to listen to and see firsthand the faith that many of these families exhibit. The witness of these families has affected me deeply."

Although Bush always began such encounters intending to console the mourners, he often ended up being the one consoled. "I marvel— I tell them often that the comforter in chief is also the comforted," Bush told me. "Many of them want to comfort me, which is a remarkable act of giving. I ascribe that to the influence of God, in many cases. There have been times when families have said, you know, 'It's caused me to question my faith.' And I fully understand that. And my prayer to them would be that I would hope that they would be able to find the comfort of faith."

Rove confirmed the importance of faith in such encounters. "I've been with him a number of times when he has met families of the fallen," Rove told me. "He talks virtually every week with somebody who's lost someone. And I think his faith helps to sustain him and give him what is necessary to go through tough times. And it gives him the ability in those kinds of situations to find compassion and, you know, to weep and cry and pray and laugh and reminisce and share conversation about a loved one. It really gives him great strength. I know it's important for him to do his job. I think it's also important for the people that he is with. That he has that strength that he can share. And that they, in turn, can share their sorrow with him."

The mainstream media, however, remained deeply skeptical.

"Is President Bush a religious zealot, or does he just pander to that crowd?" liberal writer Bill Keller asked in the opening sentence of a *New York Times* article published just weeks before Keller was elevated to executive editor. "I understand the critics' discomfort with Mr. Bush's public piety. It contributes to an image of crusading arrogance abroad, and to a fear of invasive moralism at home."

Keller fairly oozed condescension as he archly described the president as adhering to "a tradition in which religion is more a matter of the heart than the intellect. I've long suspected the essential fact about Mr. Bush is that God was his twelve-step program," he sniffed. "At the age of forty, Mr. Bush beat a drinking problem by surrendering to a powerful religious experience, reinforced by Bible study with friends. This kind of born-again epiphany is common in much of America—the red-state version of psychotherapy—and it creates the kind of faith that is not beset by doubt because the believer knows his life got better in the bargain."

It was precisely the sort of elitism made infamous by the *Washington Post* back in 1993, when a front-page news article derided evangelical Christians as "largely poor, uneducated and easy to command."

Contrary to Keller's rant, Bush displayed no more "public piety" than previous presidents, including Democrat Bill Clinton, who was forever invoking God and scripture.

"It's a religious country and our politicians tend to reflect the values of the country—that's how you get elected," Dr. John Green of the University of Akron, an expert on religion in politics, told me. "Bush has probably been criticized more for it than Clinton was, partly because a lot of the people who disagree with President Bush's policies also disagree with the policies that are being advocated by evangelicals. So it's easy for them to sort of conflate those two things."

Such critics were well known to White House chief of staff Josh Bolten. "The misperception is that he is essentially an intolerant bigot, which is the cartoon view that especially many Jews in America have of fundamentalist Christians," Bolten told me. "I can speak as a Jew on his staff. For many years, this was an enormous shock to many of my Jewish friends, because the cartoon of the president was as a fundamentalist, intolerant, born-again Christian. And he and Mrs. Bush couldn't be more tolerant."

Bolten cited a small example: whenever he dined with the Bushes, they always made sure he had kosher food, even if they were just barbecuing ribs on the grill down in Texas. "They're always very considerate about that kind of thing," he said. "They invite me to say grace much more often than the average guest because they like having grace in Hebrew on regular occasions. So they're very tolerant and certainly not proselytizing or even faintly sort of condescending in any way, which sometimes people of faith can be—you know, they're so confident in their faith and somehow you've missed it."

Although proselytizing is another defining characteristic of evangelical Christians, Bush took a laissez-faire attitude toward other people's religions, or lack thereof. And despite his abiding personal faith, he rarely viewed policy decisions through an exclusively religious prism.

"I don't think his faith leads him to many policy positions," Bolten said. "There are a couple. I think he dissected the stem cell issue very much from the foundation of his core religious beliefs. But I think those issues have been pretty rare. I think the more important influence of his faith is in the comfort and confidence it gives him to follow his own moral compass."

Rove agreed Bush's faith "gives him enormous personal strength to deal with the awesome pressures of the job." But Rove saw evidence of that faith in many more of Bush's policy decisions. "It informs him in his approach to policy," Rove told me. "You saw it in the way he talked about welfare when he ran for governor. The typical Republican would stand up and say, 'We've got to get these welfare cheats off the rolls.' Instead, he said, 'We've got to find a way to help people on welfare lessen their dependence on government and become all that they're capable of being.' And when he talked about juvenile justice, it wasn't 'We've got to lock up the little squirts.' It was 'We've got to save a generation of young people before we lose them.' And that informs his thinking as president too. You see it, for example, in his approach to AIDS in Africa, where it wasn't merely 'I'm going to talk about this issue because it's fashionable to do so.' But 'I'm going to become engaged and find a practical, responsible way for us to confront this scourge.' You saw it in his approach to the Sudan, where his faith helped inform him that there were people who were evil, and that you had to confront that evil. And you had to stand up for the right of everyone to live a peaceful life. And it wasn't realpolitik. It wasn't, you know, 'Let me look at power relationships,' and 'Is this an important area?' It was 'Is this a moral need? A moral obligation for the United States to speak out?'"

I pointed out to Bush that it was politically "safe" for his advisers to connect his faith to issues such as AIDS, Darfur, and education. I asked him whether there was also a moral dimension to hot-button issues like Iraq and abortion.

"Of course there is," the president replied. "Life is precious. You can ascribe that to a faith, of course." He added, quoting Jesus's parable of the faithful servant: "'To whom much is given, much is required.' That is a biblical admonition which should cause individuals to support those in need, and a nation to step forward and help."

When I pressed him on the moral ramifications of the Iraq war, Bush demurred. A top aide told me the president was wary of roiling Muslims who once took umbrage at his description of the war against terrorism as a "crusade."

"Look, I have been very careful not to get into the moral arguments of war," Bush told me. "But I will tell you I think it's very important for this country to face hatred square on. We've done it in the past. And we're facing a group of people that hate and use murder as a tool to achieve political objectives. That's a practical point of view, but it also can be viewed as a moral point of view. And that is: good, decent, honorable people who aim for peace have an obligation to free people from tyranny and to confront hatred."

This urge to right wrongs impressed Ken Mehlman, who worked in the White House as Rove's protégé before becoming chairman of the Republican National Committee in 2005. "It creates in him a strong sense of justice, of belief in justice," Mehlman told me. "If you look at the things that get George Bush fired up, they are injustices. The injustice of children being passed through the system of education. The injustice of genocide in Darfur. The injustice of Arab and Muslim women. He is someone who is very motivated by a sense of correcting injustice, which is interesting. It's one of the reasons that he first appealed to me as a candidate. And it's something that doesn't get enough attention."

Vice President Cheney dismissed the notion that Bush should rein in what Keller called his "public piety." "What you see in private is what you see in public," Cheney told me in his West Wing office. "He is a man of deep religious faith. And I'm glad of that. I like to see my presidents have that kind of conviction. It's an important part of who he is. But he's not the kind of guy who ever sits in the Oval Office and, you know, makes decisions based on the notion that somehow he has received word from on high as to how much money we ought to put in the highway package this year," Cheney added. "That's not what he does. The suggestion that somehow it's anything other than a strength for him, an attribute that I think is the very heart of his character, would be a mistake."

Yet critics continued to perpetuate the "popular caricature" of a president who applied a religious litmus test to all policy decisions, according to Ralph Reed, former director of the Christian Coalition of America.

"Bush's faith," Reed told me, "did not lead in any linear or systematic way to a particular issues agenda. His compassionate brand of conservatism emphasized improving education, reforming Medicare and Medicaid, ameliorating poverty, combating AIDS and malaria in Africa, and stopping the genocide in Darfur. This was not exactly the classic policy formulation of religious conservatism when he took office. In that sense, he was far more innovative at the intersection of faith and public policy than is generally understood." Reed said the president's religious conviction was strengthened in the course of prosecuting the global war against terrorism. "Just as Lincoln's faith deepened during his time in office during the crucible of a civil war, so has President Bush's faith . . . become even more profound," he said. "Lincoln said he could not imagine anyone occupying the office of the presidency who did not lead on their knees. I think that has been true of Bush."

Bush named Lincoln when asked in a December 2005 interview to cite a predecessor he had been contemplating. "I think about Abraham Lincoln," Bush told Brit Hume of FOX News. "Because you know, some of my friends from Texas say, 'Gosh, it must be a stressful time for you.' And if you really put my life in perspective . . . it's not stressful. But it's certainly not stressful compared to what a president like Lincoln went through. This was a man who was president during a civil war in which Americans were killing Americans.

And yet, during that time, his writings and his speeches reflected a man of great faith and clear vision. And so I think about him. I really do. My presidency's nothing compared to his."

Humility aside, Bush's deep religious conviction gave him a serenity that not all presidents enjoyed.

"I've seen plenty of political leaders and great government officials and politicians who, when they come under assault, begin to doubt their own beliefs," Josh Bolten told me. "But if it has to do with President Bush's core beliefs about what's right, he doesn't have that sort of self-doubt that makes people pull their punches and say things like, 'Gosh, maybe these other guys are right; maybe Arabs aren't really susceptible to democratic institutions. So maybe I'll dial back a little bit on the democracy thing for the Arabs.' His faith is very important in giving him the kind of serenity that makes it possible for him to carry through, even in difficult times."

No one accused Bush of doubting his own beliefs when he gave his audacious second inaugural address, which was rife with religious references.

"Every man and woman on this earth has rights, and dignity, and matchless value, because they bear the image of the Maker of heaven and earth," the president declared. "So it is the policy of the United States to seek and support the growth of democratic movements and institutions in every nation and culture, with the ultimate goal of ending tyranny in our world."

The speech was the "high-water mark" in Bush's "adherence to a Freevangelical faith that Lincoln, FDR, Truman, and Reagan all shared," according to writer Michael Knox Beran. "The Freevangelical policy that descends from Lincoln preserves what is best in America's messianic tradition—the belief that the United States is a 'city on a hill,' the vindicator of principles that will in time 'liberate the world'—while it at the same time prevents messianic overreach by supplying criteria for American intervention in the name of freedom," Beran wrote in *National Review*.

The "Freevangelical" label seemed particularly apt for Bush, whose belief in the rightness of his quest to democratize the Middle East was every bit as fervent as his belief in Jesus Christ as his Lord and Savior. In both policy and religion, the president was indeed a true believer.

"George W. Bush is not, strictly speaking, a politician; he came, after all, to politics late," wrote Joseph Epstein in the *Weekly Standard*. "He is instead a believer. It may well be in his nature to believe, as witness his midlife conversion to earnest Christianity. But there can be very little doubt that, on the morning of September 11, 2001, he also acquired political religion. He believes American security is being challenged, he believes this challenge must be met directly and with force, and he believes that he knows what is best for the country which he has been chosen to lead. The question of the rightness of his belief may be debated; but about the sincerity of his belief there can't be much question."

Epstein made clear that not all of Bush's predecessors held such convictions. "American presidents can be divided into those who are true believers and those who are something else: managers, politicians, operators, men who just wanted the job. While in office, Bill Clinton, who seems to have had as little true belief as any politician in recent decades, sensed that the country wanted to move to the center, so he moved to the center along with it: changing the welfare system, doing nothing radical about health care, rocking no boats, giving the people what the polls told him they wanted."

Epstein rendered a similar judgment against Bush's own father. "George H. W. Bush was a president with no known passionate beliefs. He had all his life been working on the perfect résumé: Skull & Bones, World War II hero, successful businessman, CIA director, so that the résumé's final entry, president of the United States (1989–93), was all but prefigured. But why he wanted it, apart from allowing him, when golfing, to wear a windbreaker with the presidential seal, the only logo worth possessing, is not easy to make out.

Difficult to make out, too, anything, politically, that he cared so deeply about that he would never compromise on it."

Non-believing presidents were not necessarily bad, depending upon the times in which they served, just as believing presidents were not necessarily good, depending on what they believed in and how they acted on those beliefs. Thus, in Epstein's estimation, Harry Truman, Lyndon Johnson, Jimmy Carter, and Ronald Reagan were all believers, while Dwight Eisenhower, John Kennedy, Richard Nixon, and Gerald Ford were not. As a general rule, only true believers were eligible for the coveted status of presidential greatness.

"No great American president I can think of has not been a believer," Epstein wrote. "The greatest of our presidents, perhaps the greatest American, Abraham Lincoln, was great precisely because of his deep, almost religious belief in the necessity of maintaining the Union and doing everything he could to keep it intact. Had they then existed, polls heavily in favor of his bringing the boys back home by stopping the Civil War would scarcely have dissuaded him."

Nor would Bush be dissuaded from his Iraq policy by polls showing that more and more Americans wanted to bring U.S. troops home.

"In a democracy, does a leader follow the wishes of the people, or does he lead them through the force of his own vision?" Epstein asked in conclusion. "In the best of circumstances, the political leader persuades the people of the correctness of his own beliefs. This, thus far, George W. Bush has been unable to do. But to expect him, because of this failure, to abandon those beliefs may be as unrealistic as many feel the president's own deeply held beliefs are. No one should be surprised, let alone shocked, or outraged, when he turns out to be unable to do so, and chooses to stand by his beliefs to the end."

Back at St. John's Episcopal Church, the Reverend León was wrapping up his sermon by saying that God intended humanity to be united. The minister called the terrorist attacks of September 11 a "last-gasp effort by folks in the world who want to keep people separate." Railing against such separation, León concluded, "The moment we start to speak about building a wall, they are winning."

Presently, Bush and his wife processed to the front of the church, where they knelt to take communion. As he returned to pew fifty-four, the president winked at the California kids behind him, who giggled appreciatively.

A few minutes later, Bush emerged from the "Church of Presidents" and chatted briefly with the Reverend León in front of the Doric columns. The motorcade's many vehicles were arrayed along the corner of Sixteenth and H Streets. As soon as the president and First Lady climbed into their limousine, the entire cavalcade rolled into action. Everyone in the decoy limo, ambulance, staff vans, press vans, and Secret Service SUVs were on high alert for the return trip to the White House, all of two hundred yards away.

Three minutes later, Bush was back with Miss Beazley.

Chapter Two

"THE WATERSHED YEAR"

A CROOKED SMILE STOLE ACROSS Dick Cheney's face as he pondered the irony of his predicament. Having risked life and limb to visit U.S. Marines in Iraq's deadly Anbar province, the vice president was now being interrogated by a TV anchorman who openly acknowledged the news media's "deep anti-military bias." Alas, it was shaping up to be one of those days.

Terry Moran, co-anchor of ABC's *Nightline*, had matter-of-factly explained to radio host Hugh Hewitt a few months earlier that the mainstream media's bias "begins from the premise that the military must be lying, and that American projection of power around the world must be wrong." Yet now, on December 18, 2005, Moran had no compunction about that same military providing him safe passage to Anbar province, the very heart of the Sunni insurgency, for his vice presidential interview. Moran was even using a Chinook military helicopter as the backdrop for his big scoop at the Al Asad air base, 120 miles west of Baghdad. The remote outpost was home to six hundred rifle-toting Marines who projected American power against those who had killed more than two thousand GIs since the war began in March 2003. The Marines also helped provide security for Iraq's parliamentary elections, held just three days earlier, in which a staggering twelve million voters chose the nation's first democratically elected government. Cheney called it nothing less than "a seminal event in the history of Iraq," although Moran seemed unimpressed.

"Hopes have been dashed again and again," the anchorman said dismissively. "What makes you think that this time it's going to be different?"

"I disagree with the notion that the hopes have been dashed," countered Cheney, whose smile slipped away. "I don't think that's true."

"Well, the violence has continued," Moran snapped.

Cheney tried to explain that the election capped a series of breathtaking achievements by the Iraqi people, most of whom were genuinely committed to establishing a fledgling democracy. "They've made every single milestone that's been set—every single one," he marveled. "From the time we turned over sovereignty in June of '04, to the first elections in January, then writing a constitution, getting the constitution ratified, and now national elections under that new constitution. They've had three elections this year—each one has gotten better and stronger and more effective. I do think it's serving to undermine the legitimacy of the insurgency."

As evidence, Cheney cited a "quantum leap" in the number of Iraqis telling Americans where to find terrorists and their weapons caches. As further evidence, he cited ongoing U.S. efforts to train Iraqi soldiers and police. "The Iraqi security services are clearly much, much better now," he said. "There's a big change there over the last eighteen months."

Indeed, just hours earlier, the vice president had met some of those Iraqi forces at the Al Taji air base, seventeen miles northwest of Baghdad. He had personally greeted the proud soldiers standing nervously in front of their worn-looking tanks and armored vehicles. Each Iraqi, after shaking the vice president's hand, immediately placed his own hand over his heart in a gesture of respect. Afterward, they climbed into their armored vehicles and tanks and fired up the rattletrap engines. Flashing the V-for-victory sign, they roared past Cheney, who stoically stood his ground, inhaling a snootful of dust and diesel fumes.

Standing next to the vice president was Iraqi major general Bashar Mahmoud Ayoub, who had once been imprisoned by Saddam, despite having served as the dictator's top armored commander. Heartened by the tyrant's fall, Ayoub had come out of retirement to command the newly liberated Iraqi army's 9th Mechanized Division. After watching his tanks roar away, the grizzled warrior turned to Cheney and vowed, "We will always protect against the terrorists." He then handed the vice president a small box, lined with red velvet, containing a medallion of the military seal used at the base. In broken English, Ayoub thanked America for liberating Iraq and for giving the war-torn nation a chance at democracy.

"Thank *you*," replied Cheney, clearly touched. "It's our privilege."

Although Moran had witnessed this exchange, Cheney now felt compelled to explain its symbolic importance to the skeptical newsman. "We will be able to look back, from the perspective of time, and see that 2005 was the turning point, was the watershed year," the vice president said confidently, "and that establishment of a legitimate government in Iraq—which is what that whole political process is about—means the end of the insurgency, ultimately."

Like many a journalist before him, Moran threw back in Cheney's face the usual litany of controversial statements the vice president had uttered about Iraq. The prediction that GIs would be greeted at "liberators" (they were, for the most part). The assertion that the insurgency was in its "last throes" (it wasn't, although attacks were subsiding at the moment).

Moran even trotted out the hoariest canard of them all—the insinuation that the White House had been cynically lying when it claimed Saddam was stockpiling weapons of mass destruction. Never mind that several bipartisan commissions had already thoroughly debunked this insidious falsehood.

Besides, to Cheney, all this constant agonizing over prewar intelligence and post-Saddam miscalculations missed the larger point: in the grand scheme of things, the decision to topple a brutal dictator and liberate twenty-five million innocent Iraqis was the right thing to do, regardless of whether weapons of mass destruction were ever found. In fact, Cheney ventured that even if the world had known in advance that no weapons of mass destruction existed, the Bush administration would still have ordered the liberation of Iraq. It was an inherently good thing to rid the planet of a monster with the blood of a million Muslims on his hands. Saddam had started two wars, turned weapons of mass destruction against his own people, provided safe haven for terrorists, and tortured hundreds of thousands of innocent men, women, and children.

"This was an evil man," Cheney emphasized. Mindful that the word *evil* was anathema to most journalists, who instinctively recoiled at such stark expressions of moral clarity, the vice president warmed to his theme. In clear, concise terms, he reminded Moran why we were engaged in a global war against terror in the first place, and why the central front of that war was now Iraq. "In the aftermath of September 11, after we lost three thousand Americans that morning, we were faced with the prospect that terrorists would try to acquire these deadlier capabilities to use against us," he said.

To avert such a catastrophe, the U.S. had to get out of its defensive crouch and go on the offensive, Cheney explained. No longer could Americans passively sit back and accept their fate as victims of global terrorism. The Bush administration resolved to aggressively pursue terrorists and the states most likely to sponsor them. Because

Iraq topped the list of likely state sponsors, deposing Saddam Hussein was imperative.

"We did exactly the right thing," Cheney said unapologetically. "The world is far safer with Saddam out of business. And Iraq will be a democracy," he added. "We'll help fundamentally transform this part of the world because of what we've accomplished here, what the troops are doing here, and what the Iraqis themselves are doing."

But, safely back at home, Democratic National Committee chairman Howard Dean didn't share Cheney's optimism for the future. "The idea that we're going to win the war in Iraq is an idea which is just plain wrong," Dean had concluded during an interview with a San Antonio radio station earlier that month. "This is the same situation we had in Vietnam. Everybody then kept saying, 'Just another year, just stay the course, we'll have a victory.' Well, we didn't have a victory, and this policy cost the lives of an additional twenty-five thousand troops because we were too stubborn to recognize what was happening."

Dean had called for an immediate withdrawal of half the 160,000 U.S. troops in Iraq. He had also accused Bush of lying the nation into war. "What we see today is very much like what was going on in Watergate," he railed. "It turns out there is a lot of good evidence that President Bush did not tell the truth when he was asking Congress for the power to go to war."

Impressively, Dean had managed to invoke both Vietnam and Watergate—the Left's two all-purpose templates against Republicans—in a single harangue. But his implicit comparison of President Richard Nixon to President George W. Bush had been too much for Senator Joe Lieberman, a moderate Democrat from Connecticut. Two days after Dean's screed, Lieberman reproached his own party for savaging the commander in chief during a time of war. "It's time for Democrats who distrust President Bush to acknowledge that he will be the commander in chief for three more critical years and that, in matters of war, we undermine presidential credibility at our nation's peril," he warned at a news conference.

Democrats reacted furiously to Lieberman's rebuke, ostracizing him as a pariah. Never mind that they had embraced him as their vice presidential nominee in 2000. Never mind that he had run for the Democratic presidential nomination in 2004. Lieberman was now summarily excommunicated by his own party for the unforgivable sin of defending George W. Bush.

Senate Minority Leader Harry Reid telephoned Lieberman and took him to the woodshed for not marching in lockstep with the rest of the party in trashing the president. Left-wing activist groups such as MoveOn.org vowed to recruit a liberal Democrat to challenge Lieberman, who was up for reelection in 2006.

"Some Democrats said I was being a traitor," Lieberman lamented to the *New York Times*. "It reflects the terribly divisive state of our politics."

The only people to defend Lieberman were Republicans like Defense Secretary Donald Rumsfeld and even Vice President Cheney, who had always respected his one-time rival for the vice presidency. "He is entirely correct," Cheney said of Lieberman before heading to the Middle East. "On this, both Republicans and Democrats should be able to agree. The only way the terrorists can win is if we lose our nerve and abandon our mission."

Truth be told, even the mainstream media was finding it hard to ignore the mounting evidence that, after years of setbacks, the U.S. effort in Iraq might just be starting to bear fruit. Moran's own network had actually taken a break from its unrelenting pessimism about Iraq in order to report on the historic elections three days before his interview with Cheney.

"So much pride. So much joy. The chance at a better future," marveled ABC anchorwoman Elizabeth Vargas in Iraq. "The country has never seen a day like this one before. Millions of Iraqis went to the polls in unprecedented numbers. They did so to elect a parliament which will write a new constitution and elect a new government. The Bush administration set this process into motion nearly three years ago with the overthrow of Saddam Hussein. We do not know what kind of government will rule Iraq tomorrow, but today people here had a chance to have a say in the future."

NBC News was equally effusive. "It has been, quite simply, a remarkable day in Iraq, one that could have a real impact on the U.S. mission there," said anchor Campbell Brown. "Millions of Iraqis all across the country lined up to cast ballots in today's historic elections. Even among Iraq's Sunni Arabs, as well as Shiites and Kurds, the turnout was heavy. And attacks by insurgents were light. The success of today's elections is critical to the U.S. plan for drawing down the number of American troops on the ground."

Over at CBS, anchorman Bob Schieffer was downright giddy about the news from Baghdad. "Iraq held an election, and millions voted. It really happened," he gushed. "It was, by any measure, one of the largest turnouts for a free election in the history of the Arab world."

The American public was clearly buoyed by the development, according to a poll ABC completed the day of Moran's interview with Cheney. A whopping 71 percent of respondents said the election brought the U.S. closer to the day when troops could be withdrawn. (Indeed, that same day, back in Washington, Bush himself gave a prime-time address to the nation in which he expressed hope that within a year's time, the mission in Iraq "should require fewer American troops.") The poll also showed that 46 percent of the nation approved of Bush's handling of the war, a jump of ten points from just seven weeks earlier.

Perhaps most significantly, the poll showed an eight-point spike in Bush's overall job approval rating, the largest increase since the September 11 terrorist attacks more than four years earlier. If this had been an eight-point *drop*, the mainstream media would have trumpeted it as irrefutable evidence of presidential weakness. But because it was an increase—clear evidence that the American people shared the hope and confidence in the Iraqi people that Bush and his administration were articulating—ABC and the rest of the press instinctively buried it.

Having failed in his attempt to deflate Cheney's optimism about Iraq's future, Moran switched to what he hoped would be a more fruitful line of attack. It was based on a burgeoning school of thought: the White House, in its zeal to defeat terrorism, was amassing too much executive power.

As Exhibit A, Moran cited a breathless report, published two days earlier on the front page of the *New York Times*, accusing the Bush administration of "domestic spying." The article helpfully alerted terrorists to a highly classified program of wiretapping international phone conversations between overseas al Qaeda operatives and their sympathizers in America. The revelation sent the rest of the mainstream media into an unmitigated feeding frenzy. Angered by the leak, which he said damaged national security, Bush denounced the press for undermining "a vital tool in our war against the terrorists." It was an extraordinary rebuke of the Fourth Estate by a wartime commander in chief. And yet it had zero impact on reporters, who were bent on turning the exposé into another pretext for savaging the administration.

Cheney explained to Moran that if the program had existed prior to September 11, it might have prevented the terrorist attacks. That's because two of the hijackers had been in San Diego, where they engaged in phone conversations with overseas al Qaeda operatives. Perhaps those conversations could have been intercepted, and the lives of three thousand innocent Americans could have been saved. Indeed, both the press and the vaunted 9-11 Commission were forever faulting the Bush administration for failing to "connect the dots" prior to September 11. Well, now that the administration was heeding such advice and trying to connect the dots of intelligence that might prevent another terrorist strike, the media was hyperventilating about "domestic spying."

"Mr. Vice President, this is a program that surveils people *inside* the United States —" Moran began indignantly.

"Who are in touch with al Qaeda terrorists *outside* the United States," Cheney countered.

Moran soon switched to Exhibit B of his argument that the White House was amassing too much executive authority: the issue of torture. Liberals were convinced that Bush had unleashed an army of sadistic CIA operatives to indiscriminately torture terrorism suspects across the globe. "This vice president has become an open advocate of torture," the *Washington Post* sobbed in an editorial.

Cheney dispassionately explained to Moran that "torture," at least according to the Supreme Court, was defined as "something that shocks the conscience." "Now, you can get into a debate about what shocks the conscience and what is cruel and inhuman," Cheney said. "And to some extent, I suppose that's in the eye of the beholder."

If the vice president had paused at this point, the reporter might have been inspired to formulate an uncharitable headline, like "Cheney Says Torture Is 'In the Eye of the Beholder.'" But Cheney plowed forward.

"It's important to remember that we are in a war against a group of individuals, a terrorist organization, that did, in fact, slaughter three thousand innocent Americans on September 11," he said. "It's important for us to be able to have effective interrogation of these people when we capture them. And the debate is over the extent to which we're going to have legislation that restricts or limits that capability."

Moran then asked if U.S. interrogators should be "waterboarding prisoners." He was referring to an interrogation technique that entailed tying a prisoner to a board, placing cellophane over his mouth, and then pouring water on the cellophane to induce a drowning sensation and severe gag reflex. Conservative radio host Scott Hennen had suggested to the vice president in an October radio interview that "a dunk in water is a no-brainer if it can save lives." Cheney replied, "It's a no-brainer for me." Liberals seized on this vice presidential utterance as an overt admission of torture. Well, Cheney was not about to get drawn into a discussion of "waterboarding" with the likes of Terry Moran.

"I'm not going to get into specifics," he demurred. "You're getting into questions about sources and methods, and I don't talk about that, Terry."

Moran expressed incredulity. "You—as vice president of the United States—you can't tell the American people whether—"

"I don't talk about—"

"—or not we would interrogate—"

"I can say that we, in fact, are consistent with the commitments of the United States, that we don't engage in torture. And we don't."

"Are you troubled at all that more than one hundred people in U.S. custody have died, twenty-six of them now being investigated as criminal homicides—people beaten to death, suffocated to death, died of hypothermia?" Moran demanded.

"I won't accept your numbers, Terry," Cheney said. "But I guess one of the things I'm concerned about is that as we get farther and farther away from September 11—and there have been no further attacks against the United States—there seems to be less and less concern about doing what's necessary in order to defend the country."

As evidence, Cheney cited the PATRIOT Act, renewal of which had been blocked two days earlier by Senate Democrats. After the vote, Senate Minority Leader Harry Reid crowed, "We killed the PATRIOT Act!" This drew raucous cheers from a crowd of liberals at a political rally. Never mind that Reid had been among ninety-eight senators who enthusiastically voted for the PATRIOT Act in the wake of September 11. Never mind that the act broke down the wall that had long prevented vital information from flowing between law enforcement and intelligence agencies. Never mind that it gave the government the sorts of tools to pursue terrorists that had already been in place for hunting drug traffickers. The political landscape had shifted so profoundly in four years that now the Senate's top Democrat was bragging about having "killed the PATRIOT Act." Cheney was appalled that portions of the act would expire on December 31 unless Democrats came to their senses.

"People have lost their sense of urgency out there," he lamented. "That's hard for me to do, or for the president to do. We get up every morning and the first thing we do is an intelligence brief, where we look at the threats to the United States—we do that six days a week. We're well aware that there are still terrorists out there who mean to do evil," he continued, unable to resist using that word again. "They're trying their best to get their hands on deadlier weapons, biological agents or nuclear weapons to use against us. And we need to maintain the capability of this government to be able to defend the nation. And that means we have to take extraordinary measures," he said, finally reaching the heart of the matter. "But we do it in a manner that's consistent with the Constitution and consistent with our statutes. And when we needed statutory authority, as we did for the PATRIOT Act, we went and got it. Now Congress and the Democrats are trying to filibuster it!"

None of this seemed to interest Moran, who must have known how bad it made Democrats look. So as soon as Cheney came up for air, the anchorman abruptly changed subjects to another top-secret tool against terrorism that had been gratuitously exposed by the press. In November 2005, the *Washington Post* revealed the existence of U.S.-run prisons in Eastern Europe and elsewhere that had been authorized by Bush in the aftermath of September 11. It was yet another effort by the mainstream media to harm the Bush administration through the publication of highly classified secrets. It didn't seem to matter that CIA counterterrorism agents at the prisons had extracted life-saving information from the world's most notorious terrorists, including the very mastermind of the September 11 attacks, Khalid Sheikh Mohammed. The press placed more importance on protecting these terrorists than interrogating them.

"Does the United States maintain secret prisons around the world?" Moran demanded.

"I'm not going to talk about intelligence matters," Cheney said flatly.

"Secret prisons?" persisted Moran, evidently not getting the hint.

"I'm not going to talk about intelligence matters," the vice president repeated.

"Does the International Red Cross have access to everyone in U.S. custody, as we are obliged?"

"Terry, with all due respect, I won't discuss intelligence matters. I shouldn't."

"I'd like to put this personally if I can," Moran said. "You're a grandfather. I'm a father. When we look at those girls"—evidently Moran wanted the world to know that he had female offspring—"and we think that the country we're about to pass on to them is a country where the vice president can't say whether or not we have secret prisons around the world, whether waterboarding and mock executions is consistent with our values, and a country where the government is surveilling Americans without the warrant of a court, is that the country you want to pass on to them?"

Still not rising to the bait, Cheney calmly replied, "I want to pass on to them a country that is free, that is not plagued by terrorist attacks, doesn't see a repeat of the terrible events of September 11, when we lost three thousand of our people." He assured Moran that the government was taking "extraordinary steps to make certain we maintain our constitutional obligations and responsibilities, which include both defending the country, as well as defending individual liberties and protecting the rights of all Americans."

"But it's the America we grew up with," said Moran, apropos of nothing.

"Well, somehow we go through these cycles," Cheney said sardonically. "After September 11, we are berated for allegedly not connecting the dots: 'You guys weren't tough enough. You weren't aggressive enough. You didn't follow up on all the leads.' And now it has been four years: 'Gee, maybe it was a one-off event. Maybe the terrorists out there just hit us accidentally. Maybe there's nothing for us to be concerned about.'" He added, "I want my kids to grow up in a strong, free independent America, where they are safe from the kinds of outrages that have been perpetrated not only in New York and Washington, but in Madrid, Casablanca, and Istanbul, and Bali, and Jakarta—all over the globe. And we're up against a very tough adversary. And under those circumstances, we need to do everything we can to protect the American people. And that has got to be of prime concern for us. And it is."

"Even if it's changing who we are?" said Moran, still trying to force his failed motif.

"It's not changing who we are," Cheney corrected. "We've had times in the past where we've had to . . . take steps to protect ourselves. The whole argument over military commissions: should the president be able to set up military commissions to try unlawful combatants, terrorists who've committed murder or other outrageous acts against the American people? The precedent for that is FDR in World War II, who set up military commissions to try German spies who came into the United States to commit acts of terror. And they tried them—perfectly tried. It was a legal proceeding, and they were executed. Now everybody acts as though a military commission established now is somehow a brand-new development. No, it's not. It's a precedent based exactly on what was done in World War II by

Franklin Delano Roosevelt. Extraordinary times call for extraordinary measures."

Moran then abruptly changed topics again and hounded Cheney about the Valerie Plame affair—the Beltway scandal that had swept up his former chief of staff, Lewis "Scooter" Libby. Libby was facing trial, not for any sort of illegal leaking—in fact, nobody had been charged for actually disclosing Plame's identity as a CIA employee— but for failing to keep his story straight while talking to investigators and the grand jury. The media desperately wanted to believe that Libby's impending trial was about the Bush administration's conduct of the Iraq war. In truth, it was about whether one obscure staffer intentionally covered up a non-crime.

Cheney wouldn't talk about an ongoing trial, so Moran backed off and moved to other subjects, including Hurricane Katrina, which had devastated the Gulf Coast fewer than four months earlier. The feckless governments of New Orleans and Louisiana had been no match for the monster storm, which, to a lesser extent, also exposed the shortcomings of federal emergency response capabilities. Naturally, the media shorthanded this into a handy attack line: it was all Bush's fault.

"This has been a tough period for the administration," Moran opined. "Poll numbers. The hurricane and the response of the federal government that seems wanting. A lot of Americans seem angry at the administration right now. Are you back on your feet?"

"I've been sort of in and out of this business—or in it more than out of it—for going on forty years, Terry, since 1968, when I first went to Washington," Cheney said. "Every administration has ups and downs. But when you've been through that, you have a perspective on it, and there's a little less hand-wringing inside. The president is very steady through this period of time. There are always in this business good days and bad days. We deal with the toughest problems in the world. Those are the only kind that end up on the desk of the president in the Oval Office."

Knowing the interview was coming to a close, Cheney tried to sum up his argument. "I feel very, very good about where we are with respect to Iraq and Afghanistan," he said. "Tomorrow I'll be in Afghanistan, in Kabul for the swearing in of the newly elected democratically elected parliament in Afghanistan—first one they've had in five thousand years. So it's a very special time to be part of this administration. And I think we get it right more often than not. And the American people will judge us. Eventually history will judge us. But I am proud to serve. And I think we've got a great president. And we're doing good things."

"Thank you," Moran relented. "Thank you, sir."

True to his word, Cheney boarded a Chinook helicopter the next day for the spectacularly scenic flight to Kabul. At first there wasn't much to look at as the chopper flew low over the Afghan countryside— walled fields and a few squat homes, all the same drab shade of brown. But then the chopper moved into higher country, where homes were built at impossible angles into the sides of tall hills. Higher still were vast planes shrouded by dense fog. Out of this fog rose rugged mountains capped with brilliant white snow. At length the sprawling, mile-high city of Kabul appeared.

The vice president's helicopter descended to a street directly in front of the parliament building, kicking up enormous amounts of dirt and grit that stung the skin and permeated the clothing of luckless pedestrians. Although it was only twenty yards from the street to the building's front gate, the Secret Service concluded it would be too risky for Cheney to traverse that distance on foot. So he was driven in a heavily armed motorcade. Once inside, he took a front-row seat in a chamber filled with hundreds of men and women dressed in everything from business suits to burqas. They were there to be sworn in as Afghanistan's new parliament. As President Hamid Kharzai took the stage in his trademark cape and cap, Cheney pulled on headphones to hear Kharzai's words translated from Pashto to English.

"I am opening the first session and the legislative period of the Islamic Republic of Afghanistan," Kharzai began. "Thank God for providing our nation the opportunity to be in control of its own destiny. This gathering represents the assumption of full sovereignty by the great people of Afghanistan and Almighty God's blessing. Terrorism is still a threat to our country," he warned. "Afghanistan will not be a place of terrorists, and with the grace of Allah, the Almighty, it will be saved from foreign invasion."

Kharzai's voice rose as he vowed Afghanistan would never again fall under the rule of the Taliban, which had been driven from power by the U.S. four years earlier. "We realize that independence is costly. We have to pay the price of freedom. We prefer our country's independence over anything else, even if they make us defend our homeland for another thousand years. As long as one Afghan lives, this country will remain independent."

During his peroration, Kharzai became visibly emotional, his voice cracking several times as he struggled to maintain his composure. "We Afghans have the right to stand with full dignity and self-confidence in front of the people of the world and say that this immortal phoenix, this beloved Afghanistan, once again rose from the ashes of invasion and subjugation. We have the right to declare to all those who aspire the destruction of our soil, that this country will never be vanquished. May God bless you all."

Cheney joined in the thunderous applause for Kharzai, acutely aware that such a historic moment would not have been possible without the swift and decisive actions of the Bush administration. Nor would the elections in Iraq, the fruits of which Cheney had witnessed the day before. Come to think of it, in the space of twenty-four hours, the vice president had seen significant, concrete steps toward democracy in both Iraq and Afghanistan. He knew these seminal events in Middle Eastern history were the direct result of his boss, George W. Bush, liberating fifty million Muslims and staking his very presidency on the audacious goal of "ending tyranny in our world," as articulated in Bush's second inaugural address. And yet, much to Cheney's chagrin, the mainstream media stubbornly refused to acknowledge the significance of these historic achievements.

Undaunted, the vice president spent the next day touring a MASH hospital run by the U.S. military in the Lesser Himalayas of Pakistan, where an earthquake had killed 73,000 people and left 2.8 million homeless. Such altruism by American troops made Moran's admission of a "deep, anti-military bias" in the press all the more troubling to Cheney.

The vice president was scheduled to wrap up his pre-Christmas victory lap through the Middle East with stops in Egypt, which recently held its first multi-party presidential election, and Saudi Arabia, which earlier in 2005 staged its first municipal elections. Although the balloting in both nations had been deeply flawed, it represented the small steps toward democratic reform Bush had been pushing for across the Middle East.

But just as Cheney was about to jet off to Riyadh and Cairo, he learned that he was urgently needed back in Washington to break a tie vote in the Senate. And so, after relaying his apologies to the Saudi royal family and Egyptian president Hosni Mubarak, the vice president boarded Air Force Two for the long journey home.

As the 757 streaked skyward, Cheney retired to his private cabin and settled into a comfortable chair. He offered me a drink as he reflected on what he had witnessed during his whirlwind tour. Having gazed into the faces of some of the fifty million Muslims liberated by the evangelical president, Cheney was more convinced than ever of the rightness of the administration's democracy agenda. Having seen with his own eyes that Iraq and Afghanistan were moving away from tyranny—despite all the critics back home who insisted it wasn't possible—the vice president understood, deep in his bones, that the much-maligned U.S. policy was righteous. Although he was not a man given to exuberance, I could tell that Cheney took a measure of satisfaction from the signs of progress in the war against terror.

In fact, his crooked smile was back.

Chapter Three

"A Case of Some of His Juniors Overreacting"

During his tour of the Middle East, Vice President Cheney's helicopter passed directly over the Baghdad courthouse where Saddam Hussein was being tried for war crimes. Inside was a scene that would have been unimaginable to most Iraqis just a few years earlier—the dictator in the dock, finally being held accountable for his blood-soaked reign of terror. Even now, two years after Saddam had been yanked from his spider hole by American soldiers, it was difficult for many Iraqis to believe their own eyes as they watched television coverage of the once omnipotent tyrant being subjected to the rule of law. The spectacle evoked a lingering fear of Saddam that could be exorcised by only one sight: a public hanging.

The trial of Saddam Hussein was a historic milestone in the presidency of George W. Bush. Like all presidents, Bush would be judged in part by how well he fared against his adversaries. In Bush's case, his adversaries consisted of three main groups—foreign foes, domestic political opponents (the Democrats), and the relentlessly hostile mainstream media. Topping the list of the president's foreign foes were three notorious figures: Osama bin Laden, who had ordered the September 11 attacks; Abu Musab al-Zarqawi, who headed the al Qaeda franchise in Iraq; and Saddam Hussein. Granted, bin Laden and al-Zarqawi were still at large. But thanks to the evangelical president, Saddam was now on trial for his staggering crimes against humanity.

In fact, the bill of particulars against Saddam was so lengthy that court officials had to plan a dozen separate trials. Saddam was charged with killing hundreds of thousands and torturing countless others in a veritable orgy of atrocities spanning his entire twenty-four-year rule. But his first trial was for a relatively minor offense, at least by Saddam's standards — the massacre of 148 men and boys at Dujail, a town north of Baghdad. Prosecutors could actually place Saddam at the scene of the crime — a crucial piece of evidence missing in some of the weightier indictments. So it was decided that the lost souls of Dujail would serve as proxies for the multitudes Saddam had slaughtered in every corner of Iraq.

Nestled along the Tigris River about forty miles from the capital, Dujail had been a fertile town of seventy-five thousand people until Saddam paid a fateful visit on July 8, 1982. He came to drum up support for his unpopular war against Iran, which he had initiated nineteen months earlier. Children were pulled out of school and told to line the roadway before Saddam arrived. Terrified of offending the ruthless tyrant, townspeople ran alongside his arriving motorcade, waving and cheering in adulation. The crowd was dominated by women and children because many of the men were off fighting the war. Some women stepped forward to kiss the hand of the dictator, who was wearing olive fatigues and his trademark black beret. One woman let out a prolonged, high-pitched wail of ecstasy after the dictator magnanimously touched her veiled head.

Saddam visited a mosque and a clinic before stepping inside a local family's home. He sat on a sofa and caressed the shoulders of a small girl as her mother poured him a glass of water from a pitcher. Always wary of being poisoned, Saddam declined with a wave of his hand. Later, he climbed to the roof of the local Baath Party headquarters and used a microphone to address a crowd of several thousand people who had gathered below in the sweltering heat.

"I know and everyone knows that the people of Dujail are courageous," he declared. Thanking the "sons of Dujail" for their service in the war, he avoided the fact that it was not going particularly well.

When this dog and pony show was over, Saddam got back in his car to leave. But as the motorcade neared the outskirts of town, it was ambushed by seven or eight Shiites hidden in palm groves behind high garden walls. The would-be assassins fired a dozen or so shots from their Kalashnikov rifles, missing Saddam but prompting massive return fire from the dictator's bodyguards. The firefight killed most of the attackers, as well as two children caught in the crossfire.

Saddam was no stranger to presidential assassination plots—he had attempted one himself back in 1959, when he and three other Baath Party members had laid an ambush for Iraqi president Abdul Karim Qassem one afternoon in Baghdad. As the presidential motorcade approached the trap, Saddam had panicked and began firing his machine gun prematurely, prompting Qassem's bodyguards to return fire. When the smoke cleared, a bodyguard and an assassin lay dead and Qassem was wounded. A bullet had grazed Saddam's leg, but the future dictator escaped to fight another day.

This experience did not, however, give Saddam any empathy for those who tried to kill him in Dujail. Having spent years in constant fear of assassination, the dictator was badly shaken by this attempt on his life. He was taken to the local police station to regain his composure while his bodyguards pursued the surviving rebels through orchards. Afterward, Saddam returned to the center of town, where he was filmed by an aide personally questioning a young man on the side of the road.

"Where were you going?" the dictator asked while stroking his chin menacingly.

After a terrified pause, the man said, "I am fasting and was on my way to my house."

Saddam then turned to a bald man in his forties who was being held by two guards.

"Please, sir," the man begged. "I'm in the popular army."

With icy disdain, Saddam instructed his guards, "Keep them separate and interrogate them."

It was clear from the outset that the attack had been carried out by members of the Dawa Party, a Shiite group opposed to Saddam's Sunni regime and its war against Iran, a predominantly Shiite nation. In a second speech to the townspeople, Saddam called the Dawa assassins "agents of foreigners," a thinly veiled reference to Iran.

"These few shots don't frighten the people of Iraq, and they don't frighten Saddam Hussein," he said, prompting a paroxysm of applause from the desperately worried crowd. "Neither these few shots nor the artillery bombardments will deflect us from the course we are taking."

The townspeople begged Saddam not to punish them for the attack, and so he reassured them with soothing words. "We will distinguish between the people of Dujail and a small number of traitors in Dujail," he promised.

But Saddam had already sent for his half-brother, Barzan al-Tikriti, head of Iraq's notorious secret police. Wearing blue jeans and red cowboy boots, al-Tikriti showed up later that afternoon with an assault rifle. He called in tanks, storm troopers, and helicopter gunships to seal off the city so that he could begin rounding up "suspects."

Although most of the attackers were dead, Saddam wanted to make an example of Dujail in hopes of deterring would-be assassins elsewhere in Iraq. He instructed al-Tikriti to unleash a vindictive purge beginning with the arrests of Dawa Party members and then expanding to include anyone even remotely suspected of opposing the dictator's Baathist regime. Al-Tikriti set up shop in the Baath Party headquarters, imposed a curfew, and sent for two local Baath Party officials—Abdullah Kadam al-Ruwaid and his son Misher Abdullah. The pair agreed to lead al-Tikriti's guards through town and point out suspects for arrest. They were rewarded with farmland seized from those taken into custody. A total of 148 men and boys, some as young as thirteen, were directly blamed for the attack. Another 1,500 people, including women and children, were rounded up and jailed.

The suspects were taken to Hakimiyah prison, operated by the secret police. They were packed into cells so tightly that some had to take turns standing while others slept on the floor. For a nightmarish month, the prisoners were savagely tortured by Saddam's thugs. The abuse continued after the suspects were moved to the infamous Abu Ghraib prison. After a kangaroo court found the 148 men and boys "guilty" in the botched assassination plot, Saddam signed an order for the group to be summarily executed. The other 1,500 people were sent to a remote prison camp in the desert southwest of Baghdad, where many perished over the next four years.

Those who survived returned to Dujail only to find the town in ruins. Taha Yasin Ramadan, an assistant to Saddam and a former vice president of Iraq, had ordered bulldozers to raze buildings, uproot date palm orchards, and tear up a quarter million acres of valuable farmland. Such was the vindictiveness of Iraq's megalomaniacal despot.

That vindictiveness would go unchecked for decades, of course, until Saddam was finally deposed by President Bush in April 2003.

The dictator managed to slip out of Baghdad and remain on the lam for months, narrowly escaping several missile strikes ordered by Bush. But Saddam's luck ran out on December 13, 2003, when U.S. soldiers dragged him from a spider hole where he had been hiding near his hometown of Tikrit. Back in Washington, a reporter asked Bush for his message to the captured dictator.

"Good riddance," the president said. "The world is better off without you, Mr. Saddam Hussein. I find it very interesting that when the heat got on, you dug yourself a hole and you crawled in it. And our brave troops, combined with good intelligence, found you." He added righteously, "You'll be brought to justice—something you did not afford the people you brutalized in your own country."

Indeed, two years later, Bush's prediction was coming true. The dictator who had deprived so many Iraqis of a fair trial was now afforded one by the very population he had brutalized. Saddam was actually allowed a team of lawyers to defend him against charges in the massacre of Dujail.

One of those lawyers was American Ramsey Clark, former attorney general under President Lyndon Johnson. Now in his late seventies, the radical leftist took a break from his stateside impeachment campaign against President Bush in order to join Saddam's defense team in Baghdad.

"President Bush," Clark complained in the *Los Angeles Times*, "has manifested his hatred for Hussein, publicly proclaiming that the death penalty would be appropriate. The United States, and the Bush administration in particular, engineered the demonization of Hussein, and it has a clear political interest in his conviction."

While seething with hatred for Bush, Clark openly praised Saddam and even tried to excuse the dictator's retaliation against Dujail. "He had this huge war going on, and you have to act firmly when you have an assassination attempt," Clark shrugged in an interview with the BBC.

Despite Saddam's direct involvement in the Dujail purge, Clark tried to blame the atrocity on underlings. "He was the president of the country, he was in a war, he was a pretty busy guy," Clark told the *New York Times*. "I can see this as a case of some of his juniors overreacting."

In case this "juniors overreacting" defense was not sufficiently trivializing, Clark went on to equate Saddam's thugs to the brave men and women who protected the U.S. president. "Just look at how our Secret Service works," he said. "I've been knocked down several times when they see some kind of threat."

Clark was more interested in the prosecution of American GIs and policymakers than Saddam and the seven underlings who were also charged in the Dujail massacre. "Any court that considers criminal charges against Saddam Hussein must have the power and the mandate to consider charges against leaders and military personnel of the U.S., Britain, and the other nations that participated in the aggression against Iraq," he argued in the *Los Angeles Times*.

Bush had always refused to allow Americans to be tried by foreign tribunals, such as the UN's International Criminal Court, and so the notion of GIs being tried by the Iraqi Special Tribunal was never seriously contemplated. Thus, Clark branded the court in Baghdad "illegitimate," saying it had been created by "an illegal occupying power." "The United States has already destroyed any hope of legitimacy, fairness, or even decency by its treatment and isolation of the former president and its creation of the Iraqi Special Tribunal to try him," Clark wrote in the *Los Angeles Times*. "International law requires that every criminal court be competent, independent, and impartial. The Iraqi Special Tribunal lacks all of these essential qualities."

When Clark showed up at the courthouse in Baghdad in December 2005, he was forbidden by the judge, Rizgar Muhammad Amin, from challenging the tribunal's legitimacy. So Clark led the other four

lawyers on Saddam's defense team in a walkout. At first Amin threatened to find new lawyers for Saddam, but after a brief recess, he
agreed to give Clark exactly five minutes to make his case against the
court. Further indulging the defense team, the judge then allowed
another lawyer, Najeeb al-Nuaimi of Qatar, an additional ten minutes
to assail the court's legitimacy. But Amin's patience ran out when al-
Nuaimi played the nationalism card.

"We think this land has become more American than Arab," the
lawyer railed.

"This land is Iraqi, not American," the judge shot back.

Moments later, the first witness was called to testify. Ahmed Hassan Mohammed stood less than ten feet from the dictator who
slaughtered his family nearly a quarter century earlier. While most
witnesses opted to testify from behind a screen with their voices electronically altered to preserve anonymity, Mohammed insisted on
accusing Saddam face-to-face. The bearded, bespectacled witness
electrified the courtroom with his harrowing account of being
arrested in Dujail at the age of fifteen.

"I heard a knock on the door and secret service people came in,"
he said. "People were taken to prison and most were killed there. The
scene was frightening. Even women with babies were arrested."
Mohammed and his family were taken to an intelligence facility in
Baghdad run by al-Tikriti. "I swear by God I walked by a room and on
my left I saw a grinder with blood coming out of it and human hair
underneath," Mohammed said. "One man was shot in the leg with
two bullets. Some people were crippled because they had their arms
and legs broken."

"It's a lie!" shouted al-Tikriti, who was sitting behind Saddam.

"You killed a fourteen-year-old boy," insisted Mohammed, brandishing a framed photo of his seven brothers killed by Saddam's
henchmen.

"To hell!" al-Tikriti hollered.

"You and your children go to hell," Mohammed replied.

Mohammed broke down in tears at several points, but managed to tell the court the horrors of his ordeal. "My brother and I were in the same prison for four years, just a few feet apart, but we would not see each other," he recalled. "My brother was given electric shocks while my seventy-seven-year-old father watched." According to Mohammed, the torturers taunted, "Why don't you confess? You will be executed anyway."

The guards were every bit as sadistic to the female prisoners. "One mother told the guards, 'This baby is going to die; I need milk.' The guard said, 'If he dies, throw him from the window.' Indeed, he did die, and they did throw him from the window," Mohammed lamented.

He told of other prisoners stuffed in the trunks of cars and driven into the desert by sadistic guards who bragged of burying people alive. Back at the prison, Saddam showed up one day and personally assaulted a fifteen-year-old boy. "Saddam said to him, 'Do you know who I am?'" Mohammed testified. When the boy answered "Saddam," the dictator picked up an ashtray and smashed it into his head, the witness said.

Saddam himself now chuckled at such testimony and suggested Mohammed was in need of psychiatric treatment. When Mohammed tried to respond, Saddam told him, "Do not interrupt me, son." The dictator then turned his attention to the judge. "I am not afraid of execution," he announced. "Execution is cheaper than the shoe of an Iraqi."

Neither did Saddam think much of the court's search for justice. "The purpose of this trial is public opinion," he said.

When someone in the court referred to him as the "ex-president," Saddam shouted, "I am the current president!" He heaped scorn on the court, saying it was "made in America."

"Why don't you just execute us and get this over with?" al-Tikriti blurted out sarcastically.

But summary execution was no longer the policy of Iraq's government. So at the end of the day, Barzan and the other defendants, including Saddam, were returned to their prison cells at Camp Cropper, a facility run by the U.S. military near the Baghdad airport. Sixteen days later, they returned to the courthouse to hear more witnesses testify against them.

One was Mohammed's younger brother, Ali Hassan al-Haideri, who added grisly new details about the torture of prisoners at Hakimiyah and Abu Ghraib. Interrogators held hoses over open flames, dripping the molten plastic onto the torsos of their victims. When the plastic cooled, it was savagely ripped off, along with chunks of flesh. Faces were burned and electric shocks were administered during interrogation sessions so ferocious victims had to be carried back to their cells in blankets saturated with their own blood. Al-Haideri said he personally witnessed guards carry a dead body out of an interrogation room, from which al-Tikriti himself then emerged. At Abu Ghraib, the guards didn't bother taking the victims to interrogation rooms. Beatings were administered in the hallways so the other prisoners could get an eyeful of the fate awaiting them. The anguished cries of the men and boys tormented their sisters and mothers, held just one level up. Five women gave birth at Abu Ghraib, but none of the infants could survive the brutal conditions. The tiny corpses were wrapped in newspapers and tossed in the trash.

"There were hundreds of us, and we never knew what our crime was," said al-Haideri, who was fourteen at the time of his arrest.

Saddam interrupted this testimony to demand an adjournment so he could pray. Everyone in the courtroom knew that he had always been a hard-core secularist. When the judge refused to adjourn, Saddam conspicuously turned his chair toward Mecca and placed his hands on the Koran in his lap while al-Haideri continued to testify. It was not the only hissy fit the dictator would throw in court.

Later in the day, he leapt to his feet and began railing that America had "invented" the tales of torture, which were being dutifully repeated by al-Haideri and other witnesses. Then he began complaining about what he bitterly termed "this democracy in which the Americans have imprisoned us."

"They talk about torture," he exhorted the judge. "But don't you think it would be responsible for you to ask us, the defendants, if we have been tortured?"

Saddam wasted no time answering his own question in the affirmative, even though he had never mentioned being tortured in six full days of court proceedings.

"I have been beaten on every part of my body, and the marks are still all over me," said Saddam, whose "marks" were invisible to those in the courtroom. "We were beaten by the Americans and tortured, every one of us."

When it came time to summarize that day's court proceedings in a headline, the *New York Times* decided against something along the lines of "Dujail Victims Reveal Saddam's Brutality." Instead, the vaunted "paper of record" went with "Hussein Accuses U.S. Guards of Torture." Readers had to slog all the way to the end of the article to read quotes from officials who said Saddam was treated better than the GIs who guarded him. He had an air-conditioned room, which allowed him to cool his heels in comfort while electricity shortages left most of Baghdad wilting in the heat. The Iraqi prosecutor had even visited Camp Cropper and requested TV sets and newspapers for Saddam and the other defendants. Yet Saddam, who denied his own long history of torturing others, now had the gall to falsely accuse American soldiers of torturing him. He even whined that his cell had no windows.

"There is no sun," he lamented in court, "for Saddam Hussein."

The ex-dictator would get no sympathy from Bush, whose own father once survived an assassination attempt by Saddam. Although the younger Bush insisted to me that his motivation for toppling Saddam was not "petty revenge," he clearly took a measure of satisfaction in finishing a job that his father had begun a dozen years earlier by evicting Saddam from Kuwait.

"After all," Bush said, "this is the guy who tried to kill my dad."

Chapter Four

"Don't Be a Jerk"

A SINGLE QUAIL EXPLODED out of the tall grass and flew toward the setting sun. Vice President Cheney swung his shotgun around and pulled the trigger, not noticing until an instant later that there was a man directly in his line of fire. The man fell backward and Cheney realized he had just shot one of his hunting companions. Horrified, the vice president raced thirty yards to the gully where Harry Whittington, a seventy-eight-year-old lawyer, lay flat on his back.

"Harry!" he exclaimed. "I had no idea you were there!"

Whittington didn't answer. His face was covered in blood. Dozens of shotgun pellets had pierced his chest, neck, and right cheek. One eye was open, and he was moving an arm and leg. He was conscious and breathing, but it was impossible for Cheney to tell whether the injuries were life-threatening.

A physician's assistant ran up and began administering first aid. Thank God Cheney always traveled with a medic! Having suffered multiple heart attacks, the vice president never went anywhere without his own ambulance. But the vehicle was back at the main house, miles from this remote pasture in South Texas. Cheney was on the Armstrong Ranch, a fifty-thousand-acre spread sixty miles north of the Mexican border. He had come down for a relaxing weekend of quail hunting with old friends. And now he had shot one of them!

It was February 2006 and the White House had much graver concerns than a hunting accident. For starters, North Korea was quietly readying for a test launch of long-range missiles that could alter the balance of power in the East. Bush was determined to head off this threat with a missile defense system that would protect not only America, but also allies in Asia and Europe from rogue regimes like North Korea and Iran, both of which were developing missiles and the nuclear warheads to arm them. In fact, Bush was the first president to begin deploying a network of missiles that could shoot down incoming warheads. This extraordinary endeavor, which would help determine nothing less than America's long-term security, was akin to hitting a bullet with another bullet. And yet the only bullet that would command the attention of the mainstream media for the next two weeks was the birdshot shell that had just come out of Dick Cheney's 28-gauge, Italian-made shotgun.

Truth be told, it wasn't entirely Cheney's fault, because Whittington had approached the vice president from behind without announcing himself—a major breach of hunting safety protocol. The lawyer had been searching for a quail he downed near some mesquite trees and then abruptly changed position while Cheney and two other hunters went stalking another covey. Nonetheless, the ultimate responsibility for such an accident rests with the hunter who pulls the trigger before ascertaining that he has a clear shot. Cheney, an experienced hunter, knew instantly he had no one to blame but himself.

The ambulance arrived about twenty minutes after the accident, which occurred at 5:45 PM. Cheney instructed his medic to ride with Whittington, but the paramedics said the vehicle was already too crowded. So the doors were closed, and Whittington was driven to the emergency room of a small-town hospital forty miles away. From there he was transferred by helicopter to the nearest city of any size, Corpus Christi, where he was admitted to a hospital's intensive care unit.

Meanwhile, the deeply shaken vice president went back to the ranch house. His aides and Secret Service agents quickly notified authorities ranging from the Kenedy County sheriff's office to the White House Situation Room. Before long, White House chief of staff Andy Card and press secretary Scott McClellan knew there had been a hunting accident, although they did not know Cheney had pulled the trigger. Card called the president forty-five minutes after the accident. Half an hour later, White House political strategist Karl Rove called Bush with an update. Rove had spoken by phone with ranch owner Katharine Armstrong, an old friend who had hosted Rove at the ranch on previous hunting excursions. In fact, Whittington was the lawyer who years earlier had drawn up the incorporation papers for Karl Rove and Company, the strategist's political consulting firm. Rove now gave Bush the unpleasant news that Cheney was the one who had pulled the trigger.

Around this time, the Secret Service reached Kenedy County sheriff Ramon Salinas III, who was at a family barbecue, and asked if he would be coming over to investigate. After checking by phone with an ex-lawman who worked at the ranch, Salinas concluded the shooting was an accident and told the Secret Service it could wait until morning, when he would send over his chief deputy. Salinas did not explain this arrangement to his other deputies, one of whom showed up at the ranch later that evening after independently hearing about the accident. The deputy was turned away at the gate, and so he called Salinas, who told him not to worry about it because a meeting had been scheduled for the morning.

Meanwhile, calls were being placed from the ranch to Whittington's children to let them know their father had been shot. His wife already knew about the shooting, as she had been at the ranch at the time. She accompanied her husband to the hospital.

Several other ranch guests, including a doctor, also headed for the hospital, but had trouble obtaining reliable information about Whittington's condition. The patient was waiting to undergo a CAT scan to determine whether the birdshot had penetrated any vital organs. Consequently, Cheney received only sketchy reports for the duration of the evening, including an inaccurate description of Whittington's injuries as superficial. Obviously, there was nothing superficial about taking a shotgun blast to the face and chest. It wasn't until early the next morning that all the confusion subsided and it became clear that Whittington would be all right.

Back at the ranch, Armstrong volunteered to disclose the accident to the media. Cheney agreed, as he had not brought his press secretary or the small pool of Washington reporters who traveled with him on official business. Besides, Cheney knew the press disliked him intensely and would automatically be skeptical of his version of events. Armstrong, on the other hand, had instant credibility. In addition to being an eyewitness to the accident, she had grown up on the ranch and hunted there her entire life. Furthermore, she was the immediate past chair of the Texas Parks and Wildlife Department, which made her an unimpeachable expert on game hunting in the state.

"Seemed like the ideal way to put the story out," Cheney later told me. Besides, he was still distraught over the accident. The strain was evident to Gilberto San Miguel Jr., chief deputy of the Kenedy County Sheriff's Department, who showed up at the ranch shortly after 8 AM and spent more than forty-five minutes questioning the vice president.

"I could tell he was still upset," San Miguel told a reporter afterward. "He was very, very upset. He came, shook my hand and told me he was willing to cooperate with whatever I needed."

While the deputy interviewed Cheney, Armstrong tried to reach the local newspaper, which she figured would write a story that would undoubtedly be picked up by the national press. But when she called the newsroom of the *Corpus Christi Caller-Times* at 8 AM, she got no answer. Armstrong later remembered she had contact information for one of the newspaper's reporters, Kathryn Garcia. She left a message on Garcia's cell phone and sent her an e-mail.

Meanwhile, Cheney spoke with Whittington's wife and then made the ninety-mile journey to the hospital to visit Whittington himself. The vice president felt awful about what had happened and wanted to comfort his friend. But the old lawyer seemed more concerned about protecting Cheney from possible political fallout.

"Look," Whittington said, "I don't want this to create problems for you."

Cheney was deeply moved by this true Texas gentleman. If only that sort of character prevailed back in Washington.

In the early afternoon, Armstrong finally connected with Garcia and explained what had happened. The reporter confirmed the account with the vice president's office and wrote up a story, which was posted on the newspaper's Web site at 1:48 PM. Less than an hour later, the Associated Press issued its own version of the story. The Drudge Report Web site, closely monitored by the Washington press corps, quickly posted a link to the story and slapped on a banner headline: "CHENEY ACCIDENTALLY SHOOTS MAN DURING HUNTING TRIP." The image of a flashing siren appeared above the headline, signifying the story was a major bombshell.

White House correspondents were miffed they had missed the story. They were embarrassed to have been scooped by the *Corpus Christi Caller-Times*, which most of them had never heard of. They were piqued Cheney had not spoon-fed the story to the White House press corps. And when they realized the shooting had taken place nearly a full day earlier, they began to concoct conspiracy theories about a White House cover-up. Thus was a purely accidental hunting mishap transformed into front-page news in the *New York Times*, *Washington Post*, and countless other newspapers on Monday morning. (At least the *New York Daily News* had a sense of humor about it, with the headline blaring: "Duck! It's Dick.")

On ABC's *Good Morning America*, anchorman Charlie Gibson spoke ominously about "the growing political fallout from all this. Why didn't the White House tell everyone when this accident happened? Why did they wait so long? And did that make a bad situation even worse?"

Gibson's transparently leading questions were answered just the way he wanted by ABC's Jessica Yellin at the White House. "It took the vice president's office nearly twenty-four hours to go public with news of the shooting," Yellin complained. "That delay has prompted some speculation online and on talk radio that perhaps Mr. Cheney was hoping to cover up the incident." In other words, unable to find any evidence of a cover-up through actual reporting, Yellin resorted to the unhinged rantings of left-wing bloggers and radio talk-show hosts.

On CBS's *Early Show*, reporter Matt Cooper of *Time* magazine didn't bother with any sourcing at all when he made a politically loaded joke about Cheney. "He might have had better aim if he'd served in Vietnam," Cooper cracked.

But no one was laughing in the James S. Brady press briefing room in the West Wing later that morning. White House press secretary Scott McClellan appeared before reporters for his regular off-camera briefing, known as the "gaggle," and found himself on the wrong end of a journalistic temper tantrum.

"Why didn't we hear about it for twenty-four hours?" a reporter demanded.

"The first priority was making sure that Mr. Whittington was getting the medical care that he needed," McClellan explained. "Mrs. Armstrong contacted the local paper early Sunday morning."

"So why couldn't the press office have alerted us Saturday night, when you guys found out?"

"Well, the vice president's office was working to get that information out, and they got it out Sunday morning through Mrs. Armstrong."

Truth be told, McClellan had found out about Cheney's involvement before dawn on Sunday and had advocated prompt disclosure to the national media. But he deferred to Cheney, whom many considered the most powerful vice president in history, to handle it his own way. Because Cheney's press secretary did not give regular briefings to reporters, McClellan was now left to bear the brunt of the media's ire.

"The vice president shoots somebody accidentally—and you know this Saturday night—and you don't think that you should alert us to this?" a reporter said with exaggerated incredulity. "You're just going to defer to the vice president's office? You're going to defer to somebody at a *ranch*?"

McClellan, who tended to repeat himself during tough exchanges with reporters, explained once again that Armstrong had called the local paper Sunday morning.

"But the White House press corps didn't know until Sunday *afternoon*," a reporter huffed. "The vice president shot someone, and *we* didn't know for nearly twenty-four hours later—the *White House press corps!*"

"Mrs. Armstrong contacted the local paper early Sunday morning," McClellan repeated.

"Come on," said NBC's David Gregory. "You're totally ducking and weaving here."

"No, I'm not."

"You are, Scott."

"I'm telling you what the vice president's office—"

"We don't care if some *ranch owner* calls a *local paper*!"

McClellan suggested Gregory save his grandstanding for the regular afternoon briefing, which would be televised. "Hold on," the spokesman said. "Cameras aren't on right now. You can do this later."

"You know what, Scott?" said Gregory, the anger rising in his voice. "You may think that's cute and funny, but you're not answering the question, and that's a dodge. And don't accuse me of trying to pose for the cameras. Don't be a jerk to me, personally. When I'm asking you a serious question, you should give us a serious answer—"

"You don't have to yell."

"—instead of jerking us around!"

"You don't have to yell," McClellan repeated.

"I *will* yell!" Gregory yelled, jabbing a finger toward McClellan. "If you want to use that podium and try to take shots at me personally, which I don't appreciate, then I *will* raise my voice, because that's wrong!"

"Calm down, David."

"So answer the question!"

"Calm down."

"I'll calm down when I *feel like* calming down! You answer the question!"

"I have answered the question, and I'm sorry you're getting all riled up about it."

"I *am* riled up because you're not answering the question!"

"The vice president's office—"

"You have a White House press corps, and you may think we're being a bunch of whiners about when we find out—"

Alas, the whining by the White House press corps was just getting started. It intensified at the afternoon news briefing, which the cable news outlets decided to broadcast live. True to form, David Gregory was in high dudgeon.

"The vice president made a decision about how the public should be notified that basically is at odds with the standard practice of how the president's own press operation and this White House notifies the public—isn't that right?" Gregory thundered. "Let's just be clear here. The vice president of the United States accidentally shoots a man and he feels that it's appropriate for a ranch owner who witnessed this to tell the local Corpus Christi newspaper, and not the White House press corps at large, or notify the public in a national way?"

Again and again, McClellan explained he did not know about Cheney's involvement until early Sunday. Again and again, Gregory complained about being kept out of the loop until late Sunday.

"Wait, wait, hold on," Gregory said. "Human beings are not normally this inefficient. I mean, was the vice president immediately clear that he had accidentally shot his friend, or not? Or did that information become available later? You make it seem like there's all this information that had to develop."

"I wouldn't suggest that at all," McClellan said.

"I don't understand what took so long. What information had to trickle in?" the reporter demanded. "It doesn't seem to me that that would take an inordinate amount of time. It certainly wouldn't take twenty-two hours."

It was no use. Nothing McClellan could say would assuage the fury of the reporters, who were all baying questions at once. Gregory had to raise his voice to cut through the din.

"You've got a Situation Room here, you've got people who monitor stuff," he was saying. "I mean, the vice president knew immediately, 'Oh, no, I've shot somebody accidentally,' and it takes twenty-two hours for that—"

"And you know what his first reaction was?" McClellan said. "His first reaction was go to Mr. Whittington and get his team in there to provide him medical care."

"But why is it that it took so long for the president, for you, for anybody else to know that the vice president accidentally shot somebody?" Gregory whined.

Gregory's professed concern for the president was disingenuous in the extreme—he knew that it had taken only an hour and a quarter for Bush to learn that Cheney had shot Whittington. Truth be told, Gregory was miffed about the untimely notification of exactly one person—himself. His pique was now exacerbated by the fact that McClellan kept repeating himself.

"Early the next morning, Mrs. Armstrong reached out to the Corpus paper—that's her local paper—"

"Oh, come on!" Gregory said in undisguised exasperation.

"—to provide them information," McClellan droned.

"But that's r*idiculous*!" Gregory exclaimed. "Are you saying that you don't know within the White House? *What took you so long?!*"

On and on it went, with reporters taking a perverse pleasure in publicly referring to the vice president as "the shooter." Armed with half-truths and feverish rumors, they threw around reckless innuendo to make the tragic accident sound like a nefarious plot.

"Scott, there's a report coming out of a sheriff's deputy there who said that he was prevented from interviewing the vice president by the Secret Service," said CBS reporter Jim Axelrod. "Do you know anything about that? And is that appropriate?"

"No, I don't know anything about that," McClellan said.

"Scott, under Texas law, is this kind of accidental shooting a possible criminal offense?" another reporter hollered.

"Local law enforcement office has already commented on that and said it was a hunting accident," the spokesman said.

"Is it proper for the vice president to offer his resignation?" said Connie Lawn of the USA Radio Network. "Or has he offered his resignation?"

"That's an absurd question," McClellan said.

"Would this be much more serious if the man had died?"

"Of course it would, Connie," the spokesman said. "It would have been terrible."

"This is sort of reminiscent of the levee story, frankly," opined Peter Maer of CBS radio.

Maer was attempting to link the hunting accident to the utterly unrelated breach of a levee in New Orleans during Hurricane Katrina in 2005. This irritated McClellan, who had spent months enduring media exaggerations about the administration's shortcomings in response to the monster storm.

"I reject that," McClellan said. "I disagree with that fully, Peter. I don't know what you're referring to there, but I reject the insinuation there."

"Well, when you look at how long it took for the information in that case to get through and the information in this case to get through—" Maer began.

"I don't think you immediately know all the facts in situations that you bring up, particularly in terms of a hurricane that was unprecedented in terms of the scope of the damage that occurred," McClellan said. "So I don't know how you can leap from here to that comparison."

A favorite trick of reporters was to unleash a fusillade of overly aggressive questions and then piously report to the public that the White House was "on the defensive." Naturally, they never pointed out the White House was on the defensive solely in response to their own combative questions.

"Tonight the White House is on the defensive," David Gregory sanctimoniously reported that evening on NBC's *Nightly News*, which gave the hunting accident top billing.

The accident also topped CBS's *Evening News*, where anchorman Bob Schieffer gleefully called it "the shot heard around the world, or at least around the country." Schieffer probably would have been more accurate if he had called it "the shot heard round the media."

Reporter Jim Axelrod opined, "Think about it. The vice president of the United States shoots someone, and the general public doesn't find out for twenty-one hours. Now that's the recipe for an uproar."

The uproar, of course, was coming only from the mouths of the mainstream media. Axelrod did his best to amplify the uproar with blatant exaggerations. "The shooting took place at five-thirty PM, and the president didn't know the vice president was the shooter until eight," he said. "That's two and a half hours."

Setting aside the fact the shooting actually took place at 5:45 PM, Axelrod was embellishing the so-called delay by a full hour. He accomplished this by conveniently neglecting to explain to viewers he was noting the accident in central time and Bush's notification in eastern time.

"A rare day here," he concluded breathlessly. "And by 'rare,' we mean once every couple of centuries. Aaron Burr dueled Alexander Hamilton 201 years ago, shot and killed him. And that's the last time anyone had to provide any particulars about the vice president shooting someone."

Over at ABC, self-described liberal Democrat George Stephanopoulos opined, "When there's news involving the president or the vice president, it should come from the White House or the vice president's office." The former aide to President Clinton predicted the accident could become a "metaphor" for the Bush administration. "You're already seeing the jokes about competence—the gang who couldn't shoot straight," Stephanopoulos said. "It brings up other questions where the White House's credibility has been called into question in the past. On the other hand, Vice President Cheney has never been all that favorable anyway in polls."

As the feeding frenzy intensified, former Wyoming senator Alan Simpson, an old Cheney friend, made a prescient prediction. "When it's all through after a couple of days, people are going to laugh at the media for their overreaction," he told the *New York Times*. "This is a hunting accident," he marveled. "And they're portraying him as some sort of assassin."

Unfazed, the *Times* gave the story front-page treatment again on Tuesday, breathlessly reporting that although Cheney had paid $140 in various hunting permits, he had neglected to get an additional $7 stamp on his hunting license for upland game birds. The vaunted "paper of record" treated this revelation as if it were Watergate. Its editorial page wailed that the White House was "trying to cover up the cover-up." It falsely asserted that Bush did not know "what had happened for a very long time." The editorial neglected to point out that Bush had been told about the accident a mere forty-five minutes after it happened and learned of Cheney's involvement a half hour later. The *Times*'s White House correspondent, David Sanger, contradicted his own newspaper that same day, publicly proclaiming that Bush had learned of Cheney's mishap "relatively quickly."

On Tuesday's edition of CBS's *Early Show*, reporter Bill Plante left no doubt that the uproar was all about the snubbing of White House correspondents, not the hunting accident itself. "If it were up to Dick Cheney, he wouldn't tell us if our shirts were on fire," he complained.

At the morning gaggle, McClellan decided to start things off on a light note, hoping to smooth things over with reporters. The spokesman was well aware that the hunting accident had turned into a gold mine for late-night comics, including David Letterman, who on Monday night had read a list of "Dick Cheney's Top 10 Excuses." Number four was an allusion to the film *Brokeback Mountain*: "I thought the guy was trying to go 'gay cowboy' on me." That same night, *Washington Post* reporter Dana Milbank wore a fluorescent orange hunting cap and vest during an appearance on MSNBC's

Countdown show, where he and fellow liberal Keith Olbermann traded cracks about Cheney's aim. The *Post* published an article Tuesday morning listing jokes by numerous Democrats, including strategist Jenny Backus, who quipped, "Bush-Quail '06." So when McClellan faced reporters later that morning, he tried to say something mildly humorous about the hunting accident by connecting it to the University of Texas football team, due on the South Lawn that afternoon to accept the president's congratulations on winning the national championship.

"The orange that they're wearing is not because they're concerned that the vice president may be there," said McClellan, a UT alumnus whose necktie that morning bore the team's colors—white and burnt orange. "Although that's why I'm wearing it."

The reporters laughed good-naturedly at this self-deprecating humor. One journalist playfully parried, "When is your last day?"

Another barrage of questions about the hunting accident ensued, although the reporters seemed to have lost some of their zeal for the story. McClellan did his best to treat the matter as old news. "I think we pretty much covered it all yesterday," he shrugged. "We can go through the same thing again, but my answers are still the same."

However, when the cameras were turned on for the afternoon briefing, David Gregory came alive by dominating the beginning of the session with no fewer than a dozen questions in a row.

"Other people in this room have questions," McClellan said.

"I understand that, but I'm not getting answers here, Scott," Gregory shot back. "Don't tell me that you're giving us complete answers when you're not actually answering the question, because everybody knows what is an answer and what is not an answer."

"David, now you want to make this about you, and it's not about you," McClellan said. "It's about what happened."

"It's our briefing," huffed David Sanger of the *New York Times*. "We get to ask the questions."

Sensing that the controversy was becoming more about the press than the vice president, CBS's Jim Axelrod tried to imply that reporters were merely reflecting the public's skepticism.

"Scott, do you think that this continuing questioning about the events of Saturday indicate some kind of White House press corps not getting it and sticking to something long past a reasonable discussion of it?" he said. "Or do you think it reflects a feeling in the country that this just doesn't pass the sniff test?"

Minutes after the briefing concluded, doctors in Texas held a press conference to announce that one of the birdshot pellets in Whittington's chest had migrated to the point where it was touching the surface of his heart, causing it to quiver. This irregular heartbeat, or atrial fibrillation, was shorthanded as a "mild heart attack" by a hospital administrator, although outside doctors called that a slight exaggeration. Nevertheless, Whittington, who had earlier been moved into a step-down unit, was now returned to intensive care. McClellan had learned of the development just moments before his own briefing with reporters, but opted not to announce it because he didn't want to preempt the hospital's press conference. Such discretion was not appreciated by the White House press corps, which immediately began hyperventilating about yet another malevolent cover-up.

"Today the White House, once again, chose not to tell the public about a major development in this story," huffed reporter Martha Raddatz on ABC's *World News Tonight.* "McClellan found out about Whittington's heart attack just before the 12:30 briefing. But he said nothing to the press. In fact, even though he knew Whittington's health had taken a serious turn, McClellan went out of his way to treat the hunting accident as yesterday's news."

Over at NBC, David Gregory was equally indignant. "The White House was told of Whittington's turn for the worse this morning, before it was announced," he said conspiratorially. "But press secretary Scott McClellan failed to disclose Whittington's new condition when he faced reporters during the lunch hour. Instead McClellan brushed off new questions about the shooting incident."

Not to be outdone, CBS reporter Jim Axelrod wailed that McClellan "knew about the medical procedure and the heart attack as well. But he said nothing." Axelrod, like many reporters, portrayed the spokesman as callous for having kidded about his orange tie on the same day as Whittington's heart attack. "He was making jokes about it," Axelrod marveled. "Then he found out the wounded man had suffered the heart attack." The reporter closed with a gratuitous shot confirming how much the media's bruised ego was driving the controversy. "Mr. Cheney, never a big fan of the media to begin with, really couldn't care less what reporters think of him now," Axelrod groused.

CBS reporter Gloria Borger then attempted to broaden the hunting accident into a sweeping indictment of the Bush administration. She did this by citing a single unnamed source vaguely characterized as "close to this administration." "This source," Borger inveighed, "tells us that, quote, 'It's no longer about indulging Dick Cheney's views of press management.' Instead, he says, 'It's now about Iraq and Katrina and a range of other issues that play into the public's views of this administration's arrogance.'"

This prompted anchorman Bob Shieffer to speculate that Cheney might lose his status as the most powerful vice president in history. "Do you suppose that we'll see the role of the vice president changing?" he asked hopefully. "Maybe back to the funeral beat, [which] is what vice presidents used to do before this vice president came along?"

"Well, could be, Bob," Borger said.

By this point, the hunting mishap had eclipsed all other stories, including an announcement that day by Iran that it had restarted its uranium enrichment program in defiance of the international community. The cable news networks were giving the shooting accident wall-to-wall coverage. The broadcast news shows were making it their lead item. The *Washington Post* carried two stories on the front page of the A section, plus another two on the front page of the Style section.

And yet this was not enough for lifelong Democrat Chris Matthews of MSNBC, who argued the press was actually downplaying the story. Matthews opened his *Hardball* show on Tuesday by professing, without a trace of irony, how "shocked" he was that some newspapers had "buried" the story on the lower half of the front page, not the upper half, a day earlier.

"This was bottom of the fold in the *New York Times* and the *Washington Post* yesterday!" Matthews fumed. "I've talked to experts, they can't believe that the papers treated this as such a light issue. It only moved up to the top of the fold, front page, today in both of those journals. I find that interesting."

Even Dee Dee Myers, a Democrat who had served as President Clinton's press secretary, could not suppress a chuckle of disbelief when Matthews bizarrely asked, "Has the press been playing this down?"

Oblivious to his guest's reaction, Matthews plowed ahead. "Dee Dee, I guess this is a question of news judgment, but I was kind of surprised, to put it lightly, to see that the major newspapers on the East Coast had buried this story below the fold and it was only today that they brought it up above the fold."

"I don't think putting it on the front page is burying it, Chris," Myers scoffed. "I think that was an appropriate placement for the story."

MSNBC's Keith Olbermann tried to hype the story even further by musing about Whittington's death and then asking a guest, "Could negligent homicide actually come into play?"

The next morning, on ABC's *Good Morning America*, Senator Hillary Rodham Clinton (whose husband had been impeached for

lying under oath) accused the Bush administration of being disingenuous. "The refusal of this administration to level with the American people on matters large and small is very disturbing," Clinton
said angrily.

Reporter Claire Shipman then turned to Joe Lockhart, President
Clinton's combative ex–press secretary, well known for disclosing
scandals late on Fridays, after reporters had gone home for the weekend. He was now held up as an exemplar of candor as he accused the
Bush administration of covering up the hunting accident. "When you
hold it back, you raise a whole series of issues of why you're holding
it back and what else happened and really what else is going on in the
government that you're not telling us," Lockhart clucked. "It is PR
101 and they failed PR 101 here."

Over on NBC's *Today* show, the vaunted Tim Russert said the
hunting flap "reinforces this storyline of an administration that seems
to relish or enjoy secrecy or an administration that, in the eyes of the
national press corps, is suspect in terms of credibility." Russert
whined that Cheney refused to kowtow to the mainstream media.
"He's never one who's believed in the care and feeding of the national
press corps," the anchorman grumbled. "He doesn't seem to worry
about his image. He has a constituency of one: George W. Bush," he
marveled, as if Cheney's constituency should have been NBC.
"Unless the White House, the president, says to him, 'Mr. Vice President, you must speak publicly,' he will not."

That afternoon, Cheney broke his silence, but not because he was
ordered by the president. Rather, it was because he was satisfied that
Whittington was weathering the irregular heartbeat of the previous
day and was truly on the road to recovery. Only then did the vice president invite FOX News anchor Brit Hume to his ceremonial office in
the Eisenhower Executive Office Building, next to the White House.
In somber, measured tones, Cheney explained to Hume how the
whole thing began with a single quail that flushed and flew west.

"I turned and shot at the bird, and at that second saw Harry standing there," Cheney recalled. "The sun was directly behind him. I saw him fall," he said. "The image of him falling is something I'll never be able to get out of my mind. I fired, and there's Harry falling. And it was, I'd have to say, one of the worst days of my life."

The vice president's grave demeanor instantly shattered the Left's caricature of him as callous and uncaring. Millions of viewers could see with their own eyes the anguish on Cheney's face as he lamented "what happened to my friend as a result of my actions."

"It happened so fast," he said. "Less than a second, less time than it takes to tell. Going from what is a very happy, pleasant day with great friends in a beautiful part of the country, doing something I love, to, 'My gosh, I've shot my friend.' I've never experienced anything quite like that before."

"How, in your judgment, did this happen?" Hume asked. "Who, what caused this? What was the responsibility here?"

"Well, ultimately, I'm the guy who pulled the trigger that fired the round that hit Harry," Cheney said. "And you can talk about all of the other conditions that existed at the time, but that's the bottom line. It was not Harry's fault. You can't blame anybody else. I'm the guy who pulled the trigger and shot my friend. And I say that is something I'll never forget."

Hume pressed Cheney on the questions that had reporters so upset. Why didn't he publicize the shooting earlier? And why didn't he go straight to the White House press corps?

"Now, the suspicion grows in some quarters," Hume said, referring to his media colleagues, "that this was an attempt to minimize it, by having it first appear in a little paper and appear like a little hunting incident down in a remote corner of Texas."

"There wasn't any way this was going to be minimized, Brit, but it was important that it be accurate," Cheney insisted. "As the media outlets have proliferated, speed has become sort of a driving force—

lots of time at the expense of accuracy. And I wanted to make sure we got it as accurate as possible, and I think Katharine was an excellent choice. I don't know who you could get better as the basic source for the story than the witness who saw the whole thing."

"Look at what Scott McClellan went through the last couple days," Hume said. "There's some sense—and perhaps not unfairly so—that you kind of hung him out to dry. How do you feel about that?"

Cheney replied by acknowledging that both McClellan and White House counselor Dan Bartlett had tried in vain to convince his office to notify the national press of the accident. "I've got nothing but good things to say about Scott McClellan and Dan Bartlett. They've got a tough job to do and they do it well. They urged us to get the story out. The decision about how it got out, basically, was my responsibility."

"That was your call?" Hume pressed.

"That was my call."

"All the way?"

"All the way."

Cheney made clear he was not about to apologize to the petulant mainstream media. "I'm comfortable with the way we did it, obviously. You can disagree with that, and some of the White House press corps clearly do," he said. "I had a bit of the feeling that the press corps was upset because, to some extent, it was about them. They didn't like the idea that we called the *Corpus Christi Caller-Times* instead of the *New York Times*. But it strikes me that the *Corpus Christi Caller-Times* is just as valid a news outlet as the *New York Times* is, especially for covering a major story in south Texas."

It was vintage Cheney, refusing to kowtow to the East Coast media establishment. Any other politician would have knuckled under and begged forgiveness from the mighty mainstream media. But not Cheney. To the contrary, even in this moment of maximum contrition about having shot his friend, Cheney made a point of sticking it to the left-wing national press. To the delight of conservatives everywhere, the vice president had come out and said what they knew down in their bones to be true—that the vaunted *New York Times* was no better than a local paper in South Texas.

Despite Hume's probing questions and Cheney's candid answers, the interview was instantly dismissed by members of the mainstream media who were jealous of FOX's scoop.

"It didn't exactly represent a profile in courage for the vice president to wander over there to the F-word network for a sit-down with Brit Hume," said CNN's Jack Cafferty, who admitted on the air that he hadn't actually seen the interview. "I mean, that's a little like Bonnie interviewing Clyde, ain't it?"

On CBS's *Evening News*, Jim Axelrod sniped, "The vice president chose to make his first public comments on FOX News Channel's *Special Report*, a broadcast Mr. Cheney sees as friendly, and has turned to before." (The Media Research Center observed, "One doubts reporters presumed Vice President Al Gore was going to friendly media when he sat down with ABC, CBS, NBC, or CNN.")

On NBC's *Nightly News*, David Gregory was equally peevish. "The vice president chose to speak with FOX anchor Brit Hume, a former White House correspondent," Gregory griped. "He has been outspoken in his criticism of the White House press corps' coverage of this story."

Privately, Karl Rove was equally critical of journalists for mercilessly hounding Whittington and his wife, Merce. "One of your colleagues got on the phone and began dialing through every hotel in Corpus Christi until they got a hold of Merce at eleven o'clock at night, in her hotel room, and wouldn't get off the phone—kept badgering her," Rove told me in his West Wing office. "Please. Are there any limits to decency?"

Other journalistic vultures came to Corpus Christi determined to interrogate the injured man himself. "They all felt the competitive pressure to camp out in front of the Nueces County Hospital and harass. I'll never forget it," Rove told me. "I was shocked."

Whittington knew if he railed against these reporters, it would only add fuel to the controversy. So he opted to flatter them so blatantly that everyone would know he was being ironic. Finally appearing before the vultures who had been circling the hospital for six days, the old Texas lawyer laid it on pretty thick.

"All of you in the media have been very patient in waiting for me to make my appearance here," he said with a straight face. "I hope you understand. I'm sorry I delayed you, but I know your role is to get the news out to the public. I compliment you on what you've done. I've read and seen many of your reports, and I know your job isn't easy."

He then took a veiled swipe at journalists who savaged Cheney for having the temerity to worry about his friend before worrying about the press. "I also thank all of you for understanding—the best you can—that medical attention was very important to someone my age," he deadpanned. "And you haven't failed to give my age."

Alluding to journalistic ignorance about the dangers of hunting, Whittington lamented the accident was "not easy to explain—especially to those who are not familiar with the great sport of quail hunting. . . . We all assume certain risks in whatever we do, whatever activities we pursue," he shrugged. "And regardless of how experienced, careful, and dedicated we are, accidents do and will happen. And that's what happened last Friday." Finally, to the chagrin of the media, Whittington refused to criticize Cheney. To the contrary, he heaped praise on the vice president. "My family and I are deeply sorry for all that Vice President Cheney has had to go through this past week. We send our love and respect to them as they deal with situations that are much more serious than what we've had this week. And we hope that he will continue to come to Texas and seek the relaxation that he deserves."

Impervious to Whittington's subtle rebuke, NBC's David Gregory interpreted the old man's remarks as nothing less than full vindication of the media, which by now was being heavily criticized for its over-the-top coverage of the accident. "Harry Whittington left the hospital in Texas today and, ironically, began his remarks by thanking the news media for its coverage of this incident," Gregory gloated at the beginning of his televised report that evening.

Whittington could only chuckle at such coverage.

"I talked to him afterwards and said, 'You really did great," Rove told me. "He said, 'I really enjoyed the fact that I insulted the press and they didn't seem to understand that I'd insulted them.' He was basically saying, 'You insufferable jerks.'"

Only later did it dawn on Gregory that he and the rest of the mainstream media had indeed gone too far. He admitted as much during an appearance on NBC's *Meet the Press*, after host Tim Russert read the transcript of Gregory calling McClellan a jerk in that first gaggle following the accident.

"I made a mistake," Gregory said. "It was inappropriate for me to lose my cool with the press secretary representing the president. I don't think it was professional of me. I was frustrated, I said what I said, but I think that you should never speak that way, as my wife reminded me, number one. And number two, I think it created a diversion from some of the serious questions in the story, so I regret that. I was wrong, and I apologize."

Gregory had to admit the press ended up playing the villain in the overblown story of Dick Cheney's hunting accident. "The debate playing out in the blogosphere, cable airwaves, and on talk radio pits the vice president against an allegedly left-wing, overly cynical, prissy White House press corps in a tizzy because it wasn't the first to know and angry because it hates the president and vice president anyway," Gregory fumed in a blog posting.

That was actually a pretty truthful description of the whole sorry episode, minus the qualifier "allegedly."

Gregory went on to admit he and the rest of the White House press corps had been heartless in their treatment of a man clearly anguished over having shot his friend. "One of the things we may have missed this week is a little bit more empathy for the vice president, given what he went through," Gregory conceded. "This is a terrible incident for two people, one of whom happened to be the vice president. I think we missed that a little bit in all of this questioning. I do think the vice president gave voice to that personal pain extremely well this week."

Alas, it was too late for the mainstream media to redeem itself. The American public had already been repulsed by the over-the-top headlines like the one on *Newsweek*'s cover: "He peppered a man in the face, but didn't tell his boss. Inside Dick Cheney's dark, secretive mind-set." Incredibly, the mainstream media had managed to turn a routine story about a hunting accident—while war raged in Iraq and the terrorist group Hamas was taking control of the Palestinian parliament—into a sordid spectacle of its own wretched excess. Reporters were admitting as much within a week of the shooting.

On CNN's *Reliable Sources*, reporter Candy Crowley conceded there had been "excesses" in coverage of the hunting accident, but attributed them to pent-up frustrations with "a not very media-friendly vice president." She acknowledged that journalists lost face by complaining that Cheney was secretive. "Look, there is no way for the press corps to win this," Crowley brooded. "It's never been a winning issue when the press corps—whether it's the White House press corps or the Washington press corps or any other press corps—says, 'But he didn't talk to us.' I mean, whether it's valid or not doesn't matter. The perception is that we're whining."

Host Howard Kurtz then asked Bill Plante of CBS whether the media had overreached in attacking Cheney. "Is there any danger that it looks like the journalists are badgering him—Candy used the word 'whining'—when there is this sort of pummeling?"

"Absolutely," Plante said. "I mean, we don't come off well."

"You're being portrayed as overheated, as hating Dick Cheney, as not caring about the concerns of the American people," Kurtz said. "It looks like they've put you in a box."

"Of course they have," Plante lamented. "The vice president and the White House have both used the constant press coverage of this story as a wedge. It plays to the prejudices of the people who are pre-disposed not to like us, and it's one way to distract attention from what happened."

Kurtz then turned to fellow *Washington Post* reporter Dana Mil-bank. "Isn't it true that most journalists, and White House reporters in particular, are not big fans of Dick Cheney and that is coloring the coverage to some degree?"

"I certainly can't deny it," Milbank admitted. That same weekend, he had been "taken to the *Post*'s version of the woodshed," according to the paper's ombudsman, Deborah Howell, for having dressed up in hunting garb to mock Cheney on television.

"Critics say this was showing your bias against Dick Cheney," said Kurtz, flashing a photo of Milbank in the orange outfit. "Any second thoughts about that?"

"Well, yeah, perhaps we'll skip the hat next time," the snarky reporter deadpanned. "But I was really just celebrating the colors of the Dutch national ice skating team."

"I missed that," Kurtz replied before turning serious. "Cheney says the national press is just upset because he had the ranch owner give the story to the *Corpus Christi Caller-Times* rather than to you and your self-important colleagues."

"I feel very badly about that. Look, I mean, that's the sort of pop-ulist argument," Milbank said. "And of course they succeed. The press always looks awful. They will once again make us look awful."

Cheney adviser Mary Matalin was unapologetic about the bruised egos of the Fourth Estate. "We're not trying to please the *L.A. Times* or the media," she told NBC's *Today* show. "We're trying to use—get through—the media to get to the public. And the public seems to be satisfied with the accounting that they got."

Indeed, a poll by Rasmussen Reports found that 57 percent of Americans shrugged off the hunting accident as "just one of those very embarrassing things that happens to all of us." Fewer than half that many said the incident raised serious questions about Cheney's ability to serve as vice president.

Furthermore, a CBS poll found that Americans, by an over-whelming margin of three to one, felt the media devoted too much coverage to the Cheney hunting accident. Former senator Alan Simpson had been right when he predicted that "people are going to laugh at the media for their overreaction."

Even Cheney, traumatized by the ordeal, was eventually able to look back at the experience with a certain amount of wry detachment. "The whole event was, to some extent, about the press," the vice president told me in his West Wing office. "It didn't play well, obviously, with the White House press corps, who wanted me to, I suppose, call the *New York Times* and the *Washington Post* and give them the story. So it was an interesting exercise." In the end, he seemed more bemused than upset over the media's ferocious feeding frenzy. "I didn't take any lasting umbrage at it," he shrugged. "It's a statement of the way the place works."

Not long after the accident, Cheney was in White House chief of staff Andy Card's office with a variety of senior administration officials who were debating how best to make a media splash with a development they were about to disclose.

"They wanted to get the story out and the question was, what should we do with this story?" Cheney told me. "You know, maybe we leak it to somebody first and then get coverage of it. And the debate went back and forth and I said, 'Hell, let's give it to *Corpus Christi Caller-Times*,'" he recalled. "It got a hell of a laugh."

Chapter Five

THE DECIDER

THEY WAITED UNTIL NIGHTFALL, when the sacred mosque was guarded not by Iraqi soldiers but by local police. Eight al Qaeda terrorists, some wearing the uniforms of Iraqi special forces, stormed the building in Samarra, sixty-five miles north of Baghdad, and tied up the guards. Then they set about planting explosives in a manner that would inflict maximum damage to one of the holiest shrines in Shia Islam. The idea was to destroy the mosque's signature golden dome, a century-old landmark atop a millennium-old shrine housing the tombs of revered ninth-century Shia imams. Never before had such a sacrosanct religious structure been targeted for destruction in Iraq. Even in the context of the mind-numbing violence convulsing the nation on a daily basis, an attack on Samarra's Golden Mosque was simply unthinkable.

That is, until 6:55 AM on February 22, 2006, when the explosives were detonated to devastating effect. The top of the dome was blasted clean off, exposing the Iraqi sky through a gaping hole. The portion of the dome remaining was shorn of its golden façade. Surrounding walls were reduced to rubble. And while the bombing was accomplished without spilling a single drop of blood, the streets of Iraq would soon run red.

Which was precisely what Abu Musab al-Zarqawi intended. As head of the al Qaeda franchise in Iraq, al-Zarqawi had long been trying to provoke a civil war between the majority Shiites and the minority Sunnis. He figured the resulting mayhem would cause irreparable political damage to President Bush, who then would have no choice but to withdraw U.S. forces. The pullout would leave terrorists with a safe haven, allowing them to turn Iraq into the hub of a caliphate that would one day stretch from Spain to Indonesia. In the meantime, Iraq would serve as the base from which terrorists could carry out attacks against the West. After all, if Osama bin Laden had been able to direct the spectacular September 11 attacks from Afghanistan, a landlocked, impoverished, undeveloped wasteland, there was no telling what they could accomplish from Iraq, a Persian Gulf powerhouse sitting on some of the world's largest oil reserves.

But the first step was ramping up the violence in Iraq to a level that would politically cripple Bush and America's mission in Iraq. To that end, al-Zarqawi was plotting the president's worst nightmare.

"The solution that we see," al-Zarqawi explained in a letter to al Qaeda headquarters, "is for us to drag the Shiites into the battle, because this is the only way to prolong the fighting between us and the infidels."

Up until now, al-Zarqawi's fellow Sunnis had been the primary aggressors in the post-Saddam conflict, because they were furious that control of the nation had shifted from the Sunni minority to the Shiite majority. Many Shiites tried to exercise restraint after being attacked because they were sensitive to Sunni complaints about being shut out of the political process. Al-Zarqawi calculated that if this restraint could be shattered, all hell would break loose.

"If we succeed in dragging them into the arena of sectarian war, it will become possible to awaken the inattentive Sunnis," al-Zarqawi wrote in his letter, which U.S. forces intercepted in 2004. "Let blood be spilled."

Al-Zarqawi had a long history of spilling blood. In 1992, he was jailed in his native Jordan for plotting to overthrow the pro-Western monarchy of King Hussein. Upon his release in 1999, he tried to blow up the Radisson hotel, frequented by Americans and Israelis, in Amman. The plot failed, and he fled to Afghanistan, setting up a terrorist training camp funded by Osama bin Laden, whom he had befriended a decade earlier. When the U.S. military invaded Afghanistan in the wake of the terrorist attacks of September 11, 2001, al-Zarqawi hightailed it to Iraq, where he resumed his plots against Jordanian interests. In October 2002, he arranged for gunmen to assassinate American diplomat Laurence Foley in Amman. Nine months later, his thugs detonated a truck bomb outside the Jordanian embassy in Baghdad, killing seventeen people.

Al-Zarqawi was eventually promoted to the head of al Qaeda in Mesopotamia, as the terrorist franchise was known in Iraq, and broadened his portfolio in August 2003 by bombing the United Nations headquarters in Baghdad. The blast killed twenty-two people, including UN envoy Sérgio Vieira de Mello, a high-ranking diplomat who was viewed as a potential future secretary-general of the world body. In 2004, al-Zarqawi personally decapitated Nick Berg, an American contractor in Iraq, and distributed a videotape of the grisly killing. He also orchestrated a string of bombings that killed thousands of innocent men, women, and children all over Iraq. By 2004, *Newsweek* concluded that "al-Zarqawi appears to have eclipsed Osama bin Laden as the single most dangerous threat to U.S. interests in the world today." The U.S. government put a $25 million bounty on his head, making him the most wanted man in all of Iraq. On several occasions, American forces came within minutes of killing or capturing the terrorist, whose narrow escapes merely served to burnish his status as an almost mythical figure. Bin Laden himself hailed al-Zarqawi as "the prince of al Qaeda in Iraq" and urged jihadists in a 2004 speech "to listen to him and obey him in his good deeds." In 2005, al-Zarqawi fulfilled his long-standing ambition to blow up the Radisson in Amman, along with two other hotels. The November blasts killed fifty-seven people, including revelers at a wedding reception.

But all this bloodshed was a mere warm-up to al-Zarqawi's *coup de grâce*, the bombing of the Golden Mosque in Samarra. The brazen attack was spectacularly successful in shattering the last vestiges of restraint on the part of the Shiites. Men and boys poured into the streets, screaming for revenge. They began to kill Sunni imams and civilians, at first by the dozens, and soon by the hundreds. The violence spread across the nation as swiftly as the news spread on television.

One of the Iraqis watching TV on the day of the attack was the leader of the al Qaeda team that carried out the bombing. Haitham al-Badri had been chosen for the operation in part because he had been born in Samarra and therefore had an intimate knowledge of the city and its sacred mosque. Late on the day of the blast, he was watching al-Arabiya's news coverage of the carnage he had unleashed. A fellow Samarra native, anchorwoman Atwar Bahjat, was broadcasting a live report from a gas station on the outskirts of the city, which had been sealed off by security forces. Al-Badri and another terrorist immediately jumped in a pickup truck and drove to the gas station. When they emerged brandishing machine guns, Bahjat tried to take shelter in her news van and begged a crowd of locals to protect her. But the crowd dispersed when the gunmen fired into the air.

"We want the anchorwoman!" one of the terrorists shouted.

Bahjat's cameraman and soundman tried to reason with the attackers, which only allowed the terrorists to abduct them along with the anchorwoman. As night fell, the trio was driven into the darkness and shot to death. Bahjat took two bullets in the head and another two in the back. She had been one of the most famous TV journalists in the nation.

The Samarra bombing would prove a devastating setback to U.S. efforts in Iraq. After months of progress, including the wildly successful elections and subsequent efforts toward establishing a unity government, the nation was now spiraling into chaos. The Bush administration, however, did not immediately grasp the gravity of the situation.

"It appears that the crisis has passed," Army general George Casey, the top U.S. commander in Iraq, announced ten days after the bombing.

That pronouncement proved premature in the extreme. Day after day, week after week, month after month, the bodies piled up. Rampaging packs of Shiite gunmen roamed Baghdad, abducting Sunnis in broad daylight. The terrified victims were spirited away and tortured with power tools, pliers, and acid. Fingernails were ripped out, faces were burned, bones were shattered, holes were drilled in limbs, fingers and toes were chopped off. Then the bodies were dumped in sewers or streets or the homes of the victims' families. This enraged many formerly peaceful Sunnis, especially when the Shiite-dominated government refused to investigate—much less prosecute—many of the atrocities. Always eager to make a bad situation worse, Iran lent its support to Shiite death squads. To top it all off, Iraqi police forces were infiltrated by Shiite militias, adding to the sense of Wild West lawlessness.

Seeking to accelerate his plot "to awaken the inattentive Sunnis," al-Zarqawi posted an audiotape on the Internet that incited Sunnis to fight back against the Shiites. He singled out two Shiite militias— with close ties to the Shiite-dominated government—that were operating death squads.

"They kill men and arrest women, put them in prison and rape them and steal everything from the houses of the Sunnis," al-Zarqawi railed in a four-hour screed. "Sunnis, wake up, pay attention and prepare to confront the poisons of the Shiite snakes. Forget about those advocating the end of sectarianism and calling for national unity."

Al-Zarqawi's public harangue corresponded with private intelligence the Bush administration was gathering about the terrorist's motives.

"What he was trying to do was try to kill Shias so that he could provoke a Shia reaction against the Sunni," Vice President Cheney told me. "It wasn't just a matter of political opposition to the Shia. I think he really probably looked on them as infidels."

Whatever al-Zarqawi's motive, he managed to provoke into guerrilla warfare Sunnis who had once eschewed violence. A rash of Sunni bombings killed hundreds of innocent Shiites in crowded markets. Even peaceable Sunnis felt compelled to move out of predominately Shiite neighborhoods, just as peaceable Shiites fled Sunni-dominated areas. Iraq was splintering into sectarian enclaves.

"For two years the Shia sat there and took it and didn't respond," Cheney told me. "And then finally, after the bombing of the mosque at Samarra, they clearly did respond, and '06 became a very violent year."

The sheer volume of violence utterly overwhelmed the fifteen thousand American troops trying to maintain order in Baghdad, a sprawling metropolis of seven million people. Time and again, U.S. forces bravely entered the most violent neighborhoods and, with the help of freshly trained Iraqi troops, restored order. But there were not enough Americans to stay and maintain this order. So the neighborhoods fell back into enemy hands as soon as the U.S. forces moved on to their next mission. To make matters worse, Iraqi forces were coming under political and sectarian pressure to go easy on Shiite militias. Planned raids were called off at the last minute by phone calls from Iraq's notoriously corrupt interior ministry.

"It's not always clear who the good guys and the bad guys are," Cheney told me. "So many different groups, so many different agendas being worked here—it's the Middle East. And then you take and overlay the various ethnic and religious rivalries that are involved. Shia on Sunni. Different tribal groups. Add to that thirty years of Saddam's forever heavy-handed dictatorial rule, on top of hundreds of years of history. It's a difficult, tough, complex set of relationships you're trying to deal with here."

Now that al-Zarqawi had succeeded in creating sectarian strife between Sunnis and Shiites in Baghdad, he and other foreigners dominating al Qaeda turned their attention to al-Anbar province, their home base in Iraq. Arab and Afghani terrorists from outside Iraq attacked local tribesmen and U.S. forces across this vast Sunni desert, which Cheney had visited in December 2005. Al-Anbar became the most violent place in Iraq outside the capital. Giddy with success, al-Zarqawi released a videotape of himself intrepidly firing a machine gun in the desert. But embarrassing outtakes from the video were seized in a raid by U.S. forces, who disclosed the footage to the media. The world was treated to images of al-Zarqawi utterly bewildered by the routine jamming of his machine gun, which had to be cleared by an underling. Another underling made the mistake of touching the gun's hot barrel, only to jerk his hand back in agony.

"He's wearing his black uniform and his New Balance tennis shoes as he moves to this white pickup," Major General Rick Lynch told reporters in Baghdad. "And his close associates around him...do things like grab the hot barrel of the machine gun and burn themselves. It makes you wonder."

And yet this gang that couldn't shoot straight was quite good at inciting others to do so. Al-Zarqawi's al Qaeda operation even hatched a plot to infiltrate al-Anbar's provincial government and seize control of Iraq's largest province. If successful, such a move would give the terrorists a Sunni stronghold of more than fifty thousand square miles along the borders of three Sunni neighbors, Syria, Jordan, and Saudi Arabia. The U.S. ambassador to Iraq, Zalmay Khalilzad, warned of a larger, region-wide war pitting these Sunni nations to Iraq's west against the Shiite nation of Iran to the east. Such fears were exacerbated in April, when a trio of Sunni suicide bombers killed seventy-one people at a Shiite mosque in northern Baghdad.

It didn't help matters that Iraqi prime minister Ibrahim al-Jaafari was viewed as beholden to his Shiite brethren in Iran. He was deeply distrusted by Sunnis and Kurds in Iraq, who blocked his completion of a unity government. The process was deadlocked for months, precluding the appointment of key cabinet members. American and Iraqi officials eventually concluded that al-Jaafari was too ineffectual to govern and applied intense pressure on him to step down. Backed by Tehran, al-Jaafari resisted the pressure for many weeks before finally acquiescing in late April. He was replaced by a more independent Shiite, Nouri al-Maliki.

Back in Washington, Democrats and journalists were becoming bolder in demanding that Bush set a timetable for withdrawal. The president refused and even made clear that U.S. forces would remain in Iraq at least through January 2009, when he was scheduled to leave office. This striking revelation came in response to a reporter's question in the White House press briefing room.

"Will there come a day—and I'm not asking you when, not asking for a timetable—will there come a day when there will be no more American forces in Iraq?" asked Bob Deans of Cox Newspapers.

"That will be decided by future presidents," Bush replied, "and future governments of Iraq."

This multi-year commitment to an increasingly unpopular war took its toll on the White House staff, which sometimes appeared weary in its advocacy of the president's policies. Deciding he needed to shake things up, Bush let go of his longtime chief of staff, Andy Card, and replaced him with Josh Bolten, the White House's budget chief. Bolten, given carte blanche to make further changes, wasted no time in stripping Karl Rove of his role as overseer of policy development. This allowed Rove, a political mastermind, to focus on what he did best: winning elections. White House press secretary Scott McClellan was eased out to make way for FOX News journalist Tony Snow. But these changes did not satisfy Bush's critics, who renewed their calls for Defense Secretary Donald Rumsfeld's scalp. Half a dozen disgruntled ex-generals joined the chorus, and the *New York Times* rewarded them with a front-page story, complete with photos of the dissenters. Bush took the unusual step of issuing a written statement of support for Rumsfeld, but journalists smelled blood in the water.

"What do you say to critics who believe that you're ignoring the advice of retired generals, military commanders, who say that there needs to be a change?" a reporter asked Bush in the Rose Garden.

"I say, I listen to all voices, but mine is the final decision," Bush shot back. "And Don Rumsfeld is doing a fine job. He's not only transforming the military… he's helping us fight a war on terror. I have strong confidence in Don Rumsfeld. I hear the voices, and I read the front page, and I know the speculation. But I'm the decider, and I decide what is best. And what's best is for Don Rumsfeld to remain as the secretary of defense."

Liberal Democrats immediately began ridiculing Bush for calling himself "the decider." As far as they were concerned, it was a moniker of derision to be thrown in his face for the rest of his presidency and beyond. But when you got right down to it, there was a lot of truth to the president's claim. Regardless of whether one agreed with Bush, he was indeed making the key decisions on behalf of America. That's what sparked such vitriol from the Democrats. They simply could not come to grips with the constant realization that this relatively inarticulate Texan was actually the president of the United States, the commander in chief of the American military, and the leader of the world's sole superpower. Even more maddening to these liberals was the realization that so many Americans still supported the president, despite all the difficulties in Iraq.

For example, at a question-and-answer session with unscreened members of the public at a community college in North Carolina, a man stood up and voiced his support for Bush.

"I just wanted not to ask a question, but just to offer you a message of encouragement," the man said. "I know many men and women in this room and around our region—both Democrat and Republican—continue to pray for wisdom and encouragement for you and strength during these times. So we just want to continue to encourage you."

Bush was clearly moved by the message of support. "I cannot thank you all enough for the prayers. It means a lot to me and Laura. One of the most amazing aspects of the presidency is to meet total strangers, and they say, 'I pray for you.' They don't say, 'I need a road or a bridge,'" he marveled. "They say, 'I pray for you, Mr. President.' Thank you."

A woman then praised Bush for standing his ground on a range of thorny issues, including his defense of a wildly unpopular deal that would have allowed a state-sponsored company in the United Arab Emirates to operate half a dozen major American ports. Bush argued in vain that the deal would not endanger Americans and that quashing it would send the wrong message to Arab allies.

"I wanted to say to you, Mr. President, that on the war on terror, Social Security, the tax cuts, Dubai ports, immigration, you have shown immense political courage," the woman said. "And I really think that you will be vindicated on all of those positions—as Ronald Reagan was."

Bush demurred from comparing himself to one of the greatest presidents of the twentieth century. "My attitude about this job is: Just do my job. Say what you think is right," he shrugged. "I'm just going to tell you something about the presidency—you cannot make decisions based upon polls." He added, "It's like the Social Security issue. You know, they say, well, you shouldn't have brought it up. You know, I can't live with myself if I see a problem and [I'm] not willing to address it. I want, after eight years, to be able to walk out of that office and say I did what I thought was right."

Another man stood up and relayed the sentiments of a friend, a young Iraqi woman who came to America in 2005. "She grew up under Saddam, and she actually worked for the U.S. forces during the war as an interpreter," the man explained. "I talked to her this week. She wanted to make sure that you knew that her family that's still there is grateful, that she thinks that even though there may be terrorists still going on, that they are safer now than they ever were before. And her goal is to one day meet you to thank you in person, because you have changed their lives. Even though we might not see that in the press, their lives are much better today than they were three, four years ago."

This was too much for liberal activist Harry Taylor, a sixty-one-year-old member of the far-left group MoveOn.org. He took the microphone and proceeded to attack the president. "You never stop talking about freedom," Taylor began. "But while I listen to you talk about freedom, I see you assert your right to tap my telephone, to arrest me and hold me without charges, to try to preclude me from breathing clean air and drinking clean water and eating safe food. If I were a woman, you'd like to restrict my opportunity to make a choice and decision about whether I can abort a pregnancy on my own behalf. You are—"

"I'm not your favorite guy," Bush joked good-naturedly, prompting widespread laughter and applause. "Go on, what's your question?"

"I don't have a question," Taylor replied. "What I wanted to say to you is that in my lifetime, I have never felt more ashamed of—nor more frightened by—my leadership in Washington, including the presidency, by the Senate, and—"

A chorus of boos and jeers rose up from the audience, but Bush raised his hand to quiet the crowd. "No, wait a sec," the president implored. "Let him speak."

"I feel like despite your rhetoric, that compassion and common sense have been left far behind during your administration," Taylor said. "And I would hope from time to time that you have the humility and the grace to be ashamed of yourself—inside yourself."

"You said that I tap your phones," Bush replied. "We were accused in Washington, D.C., of not connecting the dots, that we didn't do everything we could to protect you or others from the attack. And so I called in the people responsible for helping to protect the American people and the homeland. I said, is there anything more we could do?"

The president reminded Taylor that the terrorist surveillance program had been rigorously vetted by legal experts and thoroughly explained to both parties in Congress. In fact, an overwhelming majority of Democrats refused to support Wisconsin senator Russ Feingold's resolution to censure Bush over the wiretaps.

"We're at war," the president said. "We ought to be using tools necessary—within the Constitution, on a very limited basis, a program that's reviewed constantly—to protect us."

Bush concluded by posing his own question to Harry Taylor of MoveOn.org. "Would I apologize?" the president asked. "The answer is absolutely not."

Chapter Six

GOLF CART ONE

A GREEN-AND-WHITE SIKORSKY HELICOPTER appeared over the tree line and descended into a grassy clearing at Camp David. The wash from the rotors was so powerful that the Marines and sailors standing at attention had to bow their heads and raise their gloved hands to keep their hats from blowing away. When it finally subsided, the troops marched forward and formed a double line leading to the chopper door, which opened and disgorged the dashing figure of Anders Fogh Rasmussen, the prime minister of Denmark.

President Bush and his wife, Laura, who had been standing a safe distance away, now stepped forward. Escorted by a middle-aged naval officer in dress whites, the Bushes walked between the phalanx of Marines and sailors to greet Rasmussen, who by now had been joined by his wife, son, and daughter-in-law. The president and prime minister shook hands and gave double-kisses to each other's wives. Then the group emerged from the corridor of troops and paused briefly for pictures in front of a small scrum of journalists.

"See you later," Bush told the press after the handshakes had been repeated for the benefit of the cameras.

Drenched in sunshine on this perfect Friday in late spring, the smiling president climbed behind the wheel of a golf cart. The vehicle's grille, bracketed by small presidential seals, consisted of an inlaid strip of metal with raised letters that spelled out the insignia GOLF CART ONE. The buggy was the latest in a long line of presidential vehicles—including planes, helicopters, and even bicycles—whose monikers ended with the word "One." The tradition had begun in 1953, when the plane used to transport President Dwight Eisenhower was dubbed "Air Force One." Later, whenever a president flew in a helicopter operated by the Army or Marine Corps, the chopper was given the call sign "Army One" or "Marine One." In 2003, the term "Navy One" was employed for the first time when Bush helped pilot a Navy jet onto an aircraft carrier for a victory speech about Iraq. The landing and speech were widely hailed at the time, although Democrats later ridiculed Bush for having spoken under a banner that prematurely declared "Mission Accomplished." In 2004, Bush took up the sport of mountain biking at his ranch in Crawford, Texas. A fan of the Tour de France, he was intrigued to learn that the scrum of bicyclists hurtling along country roads was called a *peloton*, which in French literally means "ball" and is related to the word *platoon*. So the president began calling his own bicycling entourage, which included Secret Service agents, "Peloton One." And now, on June 9, 2006, he was having a grand time zipping across Camp David in Golf Cart One.

Bush had grown to love this presidential retreat nestled in the Catoctin Mountains of Maryland. He had come here more than one hundred times since taking office, always eager to get a break from the bustling metropolis of Washington. It was the next best thing to being on his beloved Prairie Chapel Ranch, a 1,600-acre nirvana of dusty plains, lush hills, and dramatic caverns in central Texas. Camp David was only 125 acres, but it was in the center of the Catoctin

National Park, a sprawling forest of 5,000 acres that was adjacent to Cunningham Falls State Park, an equally vast expanse. Located just seventy miles from Washington, the presidential retreat was originally named Shangri-la by Franklin D. Roosevelt because its elevation of 1,800 feet made it mercifully cooler than Washington during the dog days of summer. Years later, Eisenhower renamed it Camp David after his grandson. Like his predecessors, Bush stayed in the main cabin, known as Aspen, while his guests bunked in smaller cabins named Dogwood, Maple, Birch, and Holly. With their roofs of cedar shake shingles over curiously rough-hewn lap siding, the rustic green cabins were a dramatic departure from the stately executive mansion of the White House. Guests hiked along heavily wooded paths on the way to Laurel Lodge, a workspace where Bush often held court in a large room outfitted with secure videoconferencing equipment that allowed him to see and hear his commanders in Iraq and Afghanistan. Security at Camp David made the White House look like a convenience store. Not that the Secret Service agents patrolling 1600 Pennsylvania Avenue were lackadaisical in protecting the president. It's just that Camp David was patrolled by no-nonsense Marines in green camouflage who brandished M-16s and confiscated camera-enabled cell phones on the rare occasions when journalists were allowed to set foot on the property. Serious as a heart attack, these Marines never took their eyes off anyone who entered Camp David, which was also surrounded by a double fence and enough razor wire to put most maximum-security prisons to shame.

Invitations to Camp David were highly prized because the president used them as rewards for his closest friends and allies. That list grew shorter as the challenges in Iraq grew longer, and so Bush had not invited a foreign leader to Camp David in more than two years. But Rasmussen was that rare European leader who had supported the U.S.-led war in Iraq from the very beginning. Even now, Denmark had hundreds of troops stationed near the Iraqi city of Basra.

Besides, Rasmussen had taken nearly as much grief from the "Arab street" as Bush had. That's because eight months earlier, a right-of-center Danish newspaper had published a series of unflattering cartoons of Islam's prophet Muhammad, including one that depicted a bomb in his turban. This sparked the great "Cartoon Intifada," in which Muslims rioted worldwide, killing more than one hundred people and torching the Danish embassies in Syria and Lebanon. Rasmussen refused to meet with outraged envoys from eleven Muslim nations, saying there was a little thing in Denmark called freedom of the press. He was burned in effigy in countless cities around the globe. In this regard, he and Bush were kindred spirits.

Finally, there was a personal reason why the prime minister was invited to Camp David. He shared Bush's passion for mountain biking and had agreed to participate in a grueling ten-mile ride through the Catoctin Mountains.

"The prime minister is going to give me a mountain biking lesson," Bush said to reporters after meeting privately with Rasmussen. "Presuming he doesn't ride me into the ground."

Although the president was less than a month shy of his sixtieth birthday, he was in extraordinary physical condition. He knew that Rasmussen, fifty-three, a fitness buff in his own right, was perhaps the only world leader who could keep up with him on the bike trail's steep inclines.

"It's going to be hard work," the prime minister said in perfect English. "But I will do my very best to keep up with you."

The leaders could be forgiven for their buoyant demeanors. Forty-eight hours earlier, U.S. forces in Iraq had finally found the quarry they had long been hunting. At 6:15 PM on June 7, in a village north of Baghdad, the most wanted man in Baghdad met his maker. Abu Musab al-Zarqawi was dead.

It was a stunning victory for the American military, which had managed to infiltrate al-Zarqawi's inner circle with the help of Jor-

danian intelligence agents. This was accomplished by capturing a
member of al-Zarqawi's network and persuading him to reveal the
identity of the terrorist's spiritual adviser, Sheikh Abd al-Rahman.
U.S. forces began tracking al-Rahman's movements. The sheikh met
with al-Zarqawi at a supposed safe house in a grove of date palms in
the tiny village of Hibhib, near the city of Baqubah. The Americans
were able to definitively confirm al-Zarqawi's presence through
another informant they had cultivated inside the terrorist's organization, al Qaeda in Mesopotamia.

U.S. military commanders in Baghdad dispatched a pair of F-16
fighter jets to circle high above the safe house while ground forces
moved in to surround the structure. Specially trained anti-terrorist
troops dropped ropes from helicopters, slid to the ground, and
swarmed over the village. Someone in the safe house started shooting at the Americans, who returned fire. Fearing that al-Zarqawi
would somehow slip the noose yet again, commanders ordered one
of the F-16s to hit the house with a five-hundred-pound bomb. The
explosion shook the entire village and sent plumes of smoke in every
direction. Just to be on the safe side, another five-hundred-pounder
was dropped on the site. The blasts killed half a dozen people in the
house, but al-Zarqawi somehow clung to life. When U.S. forces
arrived, he was on a gurney being loaded into an ambulance by Iraqi
authorities. The Americans took him out of the ambulance to admin-
ister first aid. Al-Zarqawi looked up at the faces of the U.S. soldiers
and turned away, trying to roll off the stretcher. But the Americans
strapped him in and began trying to save the life of a mass murderer
who had been responsible for the deaths of untold soldiers and
Marines, not to mention thousands of innocent Iraqis. Al-Zarqawi
mumbled something unintelligible and then expired. Yes, the vaunted
terrorist who had been anointed "Prince of al Qaeda" by no less a per-
sonage than Osama bin Laden died with a mumble. And the last thing
he saw was the face of an American soldier.

Al-Zarqawi's body was loaded onto a U.S. military chopper and flown to a secure facility, where it was positively identified through tattoos, scars, fingerprints, and DNA. This process took hours, and so there was some lag time between al-Zarqawi's death and notification of the president. In fact, Bush did not know of the terrorist's demise when he met later that day with members of Congress in the Roosevelt Room to hear their latest suggestions on Iraq.

"It would be a good idea to get Zarqawi," said Republican congressman Ray LaHood of Illinois.

"I'm with you," Bush replied, according to LaHood, who recounted the conversation on FOX News Channel.

This exchange struck some as a statement of the obvious. "There was a little snickering in the room at the time," said White House press secretary Tony Snow. "Little did we know...."

Also attending the meeting was national security adviser Stephen Hadley, who excused himself from the room after about fifteen minutes to take a phone call from Zalmay Khalilzad, U.S. ambassador to Iraq. Khalilzad informed Hadley that al-Zarqawi might have been killed in a U.S. bombing raid. As his death was not yet confirmed, Hadley decided not to interrupt Bush, even after he received a second call from Defense Secretary Donald Rumsfeld. But after the president's meeting with lawmakers concluded, Hadley walked into the Oval Office to deliver the good news.

Actually, by this time he had two pieces of good news for the president. The first was that after months of stalemate, the Iraqi parliament had finally completed its unity government by filling the last three cabinet positions—defense minister, interior minister, and national security adviser. The second was that al-Zarqawi had apparently been killed.

"That would be a good thing," the president remarked in the understatement of the day. Bush deferred to Iraqi prime minister Nouri al-Maliki to make the al-Zarqawi announcement from Baghdad, which meant the news did not break on the East Coast until the middle of the night. Hours later, when the sun came up, the president placed a congratulatory phone call to al-Maliki and conferred with British prime minister Tony Blair before heading into the Rose Garden to utter the words America had been longing to hear.

"Last night in Iraq, United States military forces killed the terrorist al-Zarqawi," Bush said. "Special operation forces, acting on tips and intelligence from Iraqis, confirmed Zarqawi's location, and delivered justice to the most wanted terrorist in Iraq."

Bush was markedly somber for such a joyous occasion, partly because he did not want to be seen as gloating. After all, he was still being savaged for the so-called "Mission Accomplished" speech he had delivered three years earlier.

"Through his every action, he sought to defeat America and our coalition partners, and turn Iraq into a safe haven from which al Qaeda could wage its war on free nations. To achieve these ends, he worked to divide Iraqis and incite civil war," Bush said. "Now Zarqawi has met his end, and this violent man will never murder again."

Having been pilloried for every misstep made by the U.S. military, including the abuse of prisoners at Abu Ghraib, Bush now made a point of heaping praise on the soldiers who bagged Iraq's top terrorist. "The operation against Zarqawi was conducted with courage and professionalism by the finest military in the world. Coalition and Iraqi forces persevered through years of near misses and false leads. And they never gave up. Last night their persistence and determination were rewarded. On behalf of all Americans, I congratulate our troops on this remarkable achievement."

But the president hastened to add that America's challenges in Iraq were far from over. "Zarqawi is dead, but the difficult and necessary mission in Iraq continues. We can expect the terrorists and insurgents to carry on without him. We can expect the sectarian violence to continue. Yet the ideology of terror has lost one of its most visible and aggressive leaders. Zarqawi's death is a severe blow to al Qaeda. It's a victory in the global war on terror, and it is an opportunity for Iraq's new government to turn the tide of this struggle."

Defense Secretary Rumsfeld, who was forever being hectored by Democrats to resign over mistakes in Iraq, also took a measure of satisfaction from al-Zarqawi's death.

"No single person on this planet has had the blood of more innocent men, women, and children on his hands than Zarqawi," Rumsfeld said. "He personified the dark, sadistic, and medieval vision of the future—of beheadings, suicide bombings, and indiscriminate killings."

So it was perhaps understandable that Bush and his biking buddy, the prime minister of Denmark, were all smiles when they appeared before reporters. Besides, now that forty-eight hours had passed since al-Zarqawi had met his maker, the president no longer felt compelled to be so somber.

"I'm thrilled that Zarqawi was brought to justice," he said. "The upper management of al Qaeda was counting on Zarqawi to help implement their vision beyond Iraq. See, it's really important for the American people to understand that al Qaeda has got an ideology and a strategy to impose that ideology. And part of the strategy is to create turmoil in moderate Muslim nations. And they want to overthrow moderate Muslim nations. They want to have their view of the world—I call it totalitarian Islamofascism. Whatever you want to call it, it is extreme, and it's real. And Zarqawi was the implementer of that strategy. And he can no longer implement. And that is helpful in winning the war on terror."

Brushing off the usual questions from reporters about when he would withdraw U.S. troops, Bush unapologetically defended his Iraq policy. "You can count on America for standing by this new government, because we're doing the right thing," he said. "And people are going to look back at this moment in history and say a democracy in Iraq helped change the world for the better."

Eager to begin his bike ride, Bush bid the reporters adieu. "Okay, thanks for the press conference. Enjoy yourselves. Get out of here," he joked.

"Are you guys going to race?" a reporter asked as Bush turned away.

"No, we're old," he chuckled. "One of us is old. I'm taking a lesson."

Bush spent the rest of the weekend at Camp David, then choppered back to the White House on Sunday night to attend an event in Washington. He was back in the Catoctin Mountains on Monday for what was billed as a two-day summit on Iraq that would culminate with a secure videoconference between Baghdad and Camp David. The much-ballyhooed session was supposed to link al-Maliki and his newly completed cabinet to Bush and his own cabinet.

On the eve of this videoconference, Bush excused himself from a Camp David gathering of his cabinet members, most of whom assumed he was heading to bed. But he was actually heading to the camp's helipad. Not that he planned on skipping the next day's videoconference. To the contrary, he had every intention of participating—just not from Camp David.

Vice President Cheney was given the task of filibustering the other cabinet members while Bush made his getaway. The handful of Bush aides in the know found it comical to watch Cheney, a man renowned for his brevity, trying to draw out the moment as Bush slipped into the presidential motorcade for the short ride over to the helipad, where Marine One was waiting to whisk him to Andrews Air Force Base. Bush then unceremoniously boarded Air Force One and flew through the night to Baghdad.

It was only the second time the president had gone to Iraq, the first being a dramatic visit for Thanksgiving 2003. Back then, Bush never left the Baghdad airport. But this time, he ventured ten miles from the airport in a helicopter that flew over some of the most dangerous, terrorist-infested neighborhoods in Baghdad. He landed in the Green Zone and met for the first time with Iraqi prime minister

Nouri al-Maliki and his new cabinet. Bush's own cabinet back at Camp David was flabbergasted to see the president on the other side of the videoconference.

Later, Bush received a rock star's welcome from hundreds of U.S. troops. He lavished praise on the soldiers for the al-Zarqawi mission, the success of which had already led to a series of additional raids around Baghdad that resulted in dozens of terrorists being killed or captured. Along the way, U.S. forces scooped up a treasure trove of intelligence that would lead to even more raids.

"You know, right after September the eleventh I knew that some would forget the dangers we face," Bush said. "Some would hope that the world would be what it's not—a peaceful place in which people wouldn't want to do harm to those of us who love freedom. I vowed that day, after September the eleventh, to do everything I could to protect the American people. And I was able to make that claim because I knew there were people such as yourselves who were willing to be on the front line in the war on terror."

The president's reference to fading memories was a veiled swipe at Democrats, some of who were demanding a timetable for withdrawing troops from Iraq. In fact, on that very day, back in Washington, Bush's old foe from the 2004 presidential election, Senator John Kerry, was demanding that most combat troops be pulled out by the end of 2006.

"We have to demand a change of policy," Kerry told thousands of liberals at a gathering dubbed "Take Back America." "This week on the floor in the Senate, I will fight for an up-or-down vote on an amendment to set a date for the withdrawal of U.S. forces from Iraq." Kerry was rewarded with rapturous cheers and applause from the same crowd that had booed Senator Hillary Rodham Clinton half an hour earlier for opposing a timetable.

"I have to just say it: I do not think it is a smart strategy," Clinton had said, "to set a date certain" for withdrawal. Raising her voice over the boos and jeers, she added, "I do not agree that that is in the best interest of our troops or our country."

This fundamental difference between Clinton and Kerry, both of whom were planning to run for president in 2008, illustrated a deep divide within the Democratic Party over whether to set a timetable. Some Senate Democrats who were up for reelection in 2006 worried that a timetable would make them look like they were "cutting and running," as Bush had been arguing. They urged Kerry to shelve his amendment for pulling out troops by the end of 2006. Kerry responded by changing the timetable to July 2007.

That change, made over a single weekend, illustrated the arbitrary nature of the timetable game. Kerry wasn't setting a date based on careful analysis of how long it might take brave American soldiers and Marines to stand up Iraq's fledgling democracy. He was arbitrarily changing his timetable from six months to twelve in an effort to assuage the political fears of his nervous Senate colleagues.

When I asked Kerry about this change in his timetable, he upped the ante by pointing out an even bigger change—namely, that at the beginning of the U.S. mission in Iraq, he opposed any timetable whatsoever.

"We didn't have an election. We hadn't had a constitution. There was no provisional government. To set a timetable in that circumstance would have been wrong. But once you've had the election, once they've accepted democracy, once they've put together a government, the only thing left to do is complete the task of security transformation. And I think it's reasonable, then, to have a standard by which they assume a sense of urgency and responsibility. I don't see that as a contradiction," Kerry told me. "My plan is a plan for success. It is a redeployment for success. My plan allows the president the discretion to keep troops there to finish their training if it isn't finished, to chase al Qaeda, which is imperative for us, and to protect American facilities and forces. What more can you ask for?

I'm talking about a redeployment that gets our troops home, the vast majority, and bulk of our combat troops," he added. "Because we've done the job, not because we're leaving them."

But Kerry's fellow Democrats weren't buying it. "They fear the latest evolution of Mr. Kerry's views on Iraq may now complicate their hopes of taking back a majority in Congress in 2006," the *New York Times* reported in a front-page article headlined "On Iraq, Kerry Again Leaves Democrats Fuming." Indeed, only a dozen other Democrats voted for the amendment, which failed 86–13. Most Democrats preferred a politically safer course set by Senators Carl Levin and Jack Reed, who vaguely called for a withdrawal to begin by the end of 2006 without any timetable for completing the pullout. All but a half-dozen Democrats voted for this nonbinding "sense of the Senate" resolution, which nonetheless was defeated by the Republican-controlled chamber 60–39.

Bush advised the troops in Baghdad to ignore all this arguing over a timetable. "What you're doing is historic," he marveled. "People will look back at this period and wonder whether or not America was true to its beginnings; whether we strongly believed in the universality of freedom and whether we were willing to act on it. Certainly we acted in our own self-interest right after September the eleventh," he added. "And now we act not only in our own self-interests, but in the interests of men, women, and children in the broader Middle East— no matter what their religion, no matter where they were born, no matter how they speak. This is a moment," he concluded. "This is a time where the world can turn one way or the other, where the world can be a better place or a more dangerous place. And the United States of America and citizens such as yourself are dedicated to making sure that the world we leave behind is a better place for all."

The crowd went nuts, and the president beamed. Soon he was back on Air Force One for the long journey home. It was hard not to feel good about the prospects for freedom in Iraq. Al-Zarqawi was dead. Saddam was on trial for crimes against humanity. Iraq's unity government was complete. Bush had sized up the new prime minister and liked what he saw. The two leaders had agreed on a new security plan, dubbed "Operation Together Forward," aimed at curbing Baghdad's violence, which had been raging since the bombing of the Golden Mosque in Samarra.

"We came away from that trip with a lot of optimism, which was genuine," White House chief of staff Josh Bolten told me. "But it was masking what was going on underneath—the radicalization of the Shia militia; the cycle of retribution that al Qaeda set out to instigate. And succeeded."

Chapter Seven

Botched Jokes

For five days, Senator George Allen managed to ignore the college kid with the funny haircut who had been filming the Virginia Republican's every utterance in hopes of catching him in a gaffe. The practice, known as "tracking," was a staple of modern politics. In fact, Allen had his own campaign worker tracking the Democratic challenger, James Webb, in these final ninety days of the campaign.

So Allen didn't take it personally when Webb dispatched S. R. Sidarth to shadow the Republican on his "listening tour" of Virginia. At first, Allen mistook Sidarth for a supporter and shook his hand at a campaign event. When the gregarious senator inquired about Sidarth's line of work, the shy University of Virginia senior replied, "Following you around." Allen smiled to signify he understood and then moved on.

Allen's aides went out of their way to be courteous to twenty-year-old-Sidarth, the son of immigrants from India. They shot the breeze with him between campaign appearances, asking if he had slept well and making small talk about the Allen-commissioned tracker who was shadowing Webb. Republicans who showed up at Allen rallies invariably insisted on feeding the quiet kid who seemed slightly self-conscious about his mohawk-style haircut, which he vaguely blamed on his roommates. Sure, he was a Democrat working for Webb, but he seemed harmless enough.

Besides, Allen had been leading Webb in the polls by double-digit margins since the race began. The popular senator was widely expected to cruise to reelection and then mount a long-planned White House bid in 2008. He certainly wasn't about to let a college kid with a camcorder rattle him as he delivered a stump speech in rural Virginia on August 11, 2006.

"My friends," Allen was saying, "we're gonna run this campaign on positive, constructive ideas. And it's important that we motivate and inspire people for something."

Clutching a microphone and wearing a blue work shirt with the sleeves rolled up, Allen scanned the beaming faces of his rapt supporters. A hundred rock-ribbed Republicans had come out to meet the candidate at a picnic in the sprawling Breaks Interstate Park along Virginia's border with Kentucky. They seemed to be lapping up this stock speech of feel-good platitudes.

But then Allen's gaze came to rest on Sidarth, who, as usual, was pointing his slender camcorder directly at the candidate. For some reason, this irked Allen. The senator had been in a playful mood, and so he began what he thought would be a harmless riff on the college kid with a funny haircut.

"This fellow here, over here with the yellow shirt, Macaca, or whatever his name is, he's with my opponent," Allen said with a smile as he waved a finger in Sidarth's direction. "He's following us around everywhere."

A lone woman in the audience guffawed. Suitably encouraged, Allen riffed on.

"And it's just great. We're going to places all over Virginia, and he's having it on film, and it's great to have you here, and you show it to your opponent because he's never been there and probably will never come."

"Whoooo!" hollered several supporters amid a smattering of applause.

"So it's good for you to see what it's like out here in the real world, rather than living inside the Beltway."

The applause now intensified, prompting Allen to pause before noting that his "opponent, actually, right now, is with a bunch of Hollywood movie moguls. We care about fact, not fiction."

More peals of derisive laughter from the crowd.

"So welcome," Allen said with a smile, looking directly into Sidarth's camera. "Let's give a welcome to Macaca here. Welcome to America and the real world of Virginia."

The crowd obliged with a final round of applause as Allen returned to his stock speech.

"My friends, we're in the midst of a war on terror," he resumed.

Sidarth kept filming until the speech was over, at which point the Republicans insisted on feeding him again. "Political differences are set aside at the dinner table," one woman explained as they broke bread at a picnic table. Others helpfully gave Sidarth driving directions to Allen's next campaign event, which was scheduled for the following morning in Bluefield, Virginia.

After the picnic, Sidarth called his superiors at Webb's campaign headquarters in Arlington, Virginia. It was late Friday afternoon as he recounted how Allen had poked fun at him. The campaign aides thought so little of the episode that they promptly adjourned to a nearby bar. Reporters covering Allen's campaign were equally unimpressed. They opted not to write a single word about Allen's remarks in the Saturday, Sunday, or Monday newspapers.

Such indifference was easy to understand. For starters, no one seemed to be familiar with the word *macaca*. And even if the word could be vaguely construed as some sort of slur against Indian Americans, other senators had demonstrated there was little political risk in poking fun at this particular ethnic group. Just a month earlier, Democratic senator Joe Biden of Delaware, also planning a White House bid, made a much more overt joke about immigrants from India.

"You cannot go into a Dunkin' Donuts or a 7-Eleven unless you have a slight Indian accent," he told an Indian American during a campaign swing in New Hampshire. "I'm not joking." Biden refused to apologize for stereotyping Indian Americans, telling MSNBC, "It was meant as a compliment."

Fellow Democratic senator Hillary Rodham Clinton, who was also laying the groundwork for a 2008 White House run, went even further by poking fun at the most revered Indian of all, Mahatma Gandhi. "He ran a gas station down in St. Louis for a couple of years," Clinton cracked at a 2004 fund-raiser in St. Louis. The audience of Democrats roared with laughter as the New Yorker mockingly pointed in the distance, pretending to recognize India's long-dead spiritual leader. "Mr. Gandhi, you still go to the gas station?" she joked. "A lot of wisdom comes out of that gas station."

Clinton later told reporters, "It was a lame attempt at humor and I am very sorry that it might have been interpreted in a way that causes stress to anyone."

The press treated the Clinton and Biden gaffes as minor kerfuffles that did not merit extensive coverage. Stories about the flaps were forgiving in tone and relied heavily on sources defending the Democrats. The *Washington Post* did not even bother mentioning the Biden episode.

But the allowances made for Biden and Clinton, both liberal Democrats, did not extend to Allen, a conservative Republican. Because the mainstream media regarded conservatives as innately bigoted, reporters pounced whenever a Republican said something that could be remotely construed as racially insensitive, and journalists structured their stories to confirm this stereotype. By contrast, the same media regarded liberals as innately egalitarian. Accordingly, reporters generally made excuses whenever a Democrat said something racially insensitive, and journalists explained away such gaffes as unfortunate anomalies.

Still, a *Washington Post* reporter was initially hesitant when the Webb campaign suggested a "macaca" story three days after the utterance. Webb aides told the reporter that Allen's remarks were demeaning and insensitive. They skillfully created a demand for the story by cryptically leaking word to left-wing bloggers that a major revelation about Allen was imminent. And then, in an inspired move, Webb officials posted Sidarth's footage of Allen on YouTube, the wildly popular Internet site for video sharing. The strategy was devastatingly effective. Within hours, the blogosphere was working itself into a froth, and the *Post*—as characterized by liberal online magazine *Salon*—had "taken the bait." A *Post* reporter phoned Allen's campaign manager, who dismissed the "macaca" inquiry as absurd. But that evening the reporter reached Allen himself, who decided to issue an unqualified mea culpa.

"I would never want to demean him as an individual," Allen explained. "I do apologize if he's offended by that. That was no way the point."

But the press was not about to extend to Allen the same forgiveness and understanding it had given Clinton and Biden in explaining away their stereotypical remarks about Indians. Nor were journalists inclined to quote sources who could vouch for Allen's good intentions. He was, after all, a conservative Republican. He must have meant it.

So on Tuesday morning, the *Post* kicked off a mainstream media feeding frenzy by running the first of what would be many front-page articles on the "macaca" gaffe.

"Depending on how it is spelled, the word *macaca* could mean either a monkey that inhabits the Eastern Hemisphere or a town in South Africa," the *Post* reporters explained. "In some European cultures, *macaca* is also considered a racial slur against African immigrants, according to several Web sites that track ethnic slurs."

Translation: *macaca* wasn't listed as a racial slur in ordinary dictionaries or encyclopedias, and so the *Post* had to dig up some obscure Web sites in order to make the case that Allen was a racist. It was a stretch, but that didn't stop the rest of the press from piling on. To bolster their characterization of Allen as a racially insensitive bully, reporters dredged up a trio of anecdotes utterly unrelated to the "macaca" gaffe.

The first was the candidate's affinity for the Confederate flag, which Allen had displayed at times dating back to his high school days. He attributed this to a youthful "rebelliousness," adding that only later in life did he realize that "the flag is seen as a symbol of repression for some—and understandably so."

The second was a noose once displayed in Allen's office as part of a Western motif that included wagon wheels and pieces of old plows. Liberals claimed the noose reminded them of lynching, but Allen countered, "It was nothing more than a decoration—law-and-order type stuff."

The third was a book written in 2000 by Allen's younger sister, Jennifer Allen, which described him as a bully when they were growing up. In a passage about one of her boyfriends, Richard wrote, "My brother George welcomed him by slamming a pool cue against his head." Richard later recanted, calling the pool cue story "a joke," and the book in general "a novelization of the past." Allen, for his part, didn't hold a grudge. "I love my sister; she loves me," he shrugged. "When she got married, she asked me to walk her down the aisle."

Two weeks after the "macaca" gaffe, I spent a day with Allen as he crisscrossed southwestern Virginia on his campaign bus. His double-digit lead over Webb in the polls had evaporated and he was still being asked about the controversy at every stop. Between campaign appearances in small towns, Allen slouched in the front seat of his bus with his cowboy boots propped on the dashboard. The son of NFL coach George Allen, the senator idly fiddled with his ever-present football, the source of endless metaphors for political leadership. He chewed a fat wad of tobacco, pausing frequently to dribble juice into a cup as he talked about the two media outlets that were leading the charge to destroy his campaign, the *Post* and MSNBC's *Hardball with Chris Matthews.*

"I don't consider them necessarily my fans," Allen said ruefully, adding they may "have a political axe to grind." But his disdain for the mainstream media was not limited to one or two news outlets. "I don't think there's any question that people at the *Washington Post* or the *New York Times* and many of these major respected newspapers have a liberal point of view," Allen said. "At times they're irresponsible."

True enough, but Allen had also been irresponsible by giving the press the ammunition to use against him in the first place. Sure, the mainstream media had a double standard, but successful conservatives were expected to cope with that well-known reality without self-destructing.

After my interview, I asked veteran political handicapper Charlie Cook to assess Allen's presidential prospects. "One year ago," Cook said, "I would have thought that George Allen would have the best chance of winning the Republican nomination of anyone. And I was saying and writing that." He added, "Today, I think there's practically no chance at all."

Because the Democrats were poised to make gains in the Senate already, an endangered Allen made all Republicans nervous. Adding to the unease, Allen was not the only Republican to become mired in controversy in the run-up to the midterm elections of 2006. Two months earlier, Tom DeLay of Texas had resigned from Congress, where he had served as the powerful House majority leader for three years. His stunning fall from power was engineered by Democratic prosecutor Ronnie Earle, who convinced a grand jury in Travis County, Texas, to indict DeLay on charges of conspiracy to violate election laws. DeLay denounced Earle as a partisan hack, but the indictment forced DeLay to give up his leadership post and ultimately to quit Congress altogether.

Also in 2006, GOP congressman Randy "Duke" Cunningham of California was sentenced to more than eight years in prison for accepting at least $2.4 million in bribes. Meanwhile, the FBI launched a high-profile investigation into reports that Republican congressman Curt Weldon of Pennsylvania had granted favors to Russians and Serbs who steered lucrative contracts to his daughter. Another Pennsylvania Republican, sixty-five-year-old Congressman Don Sherwood, was accused of trying to strangle his Peruvian mistress.

But the most politically damaging scandal of all was caused by GOP congressman Mark Foley of Florida, who sent a series of sexual computer messages to a seventeen-year-old boy who worked as a congressional page. When the messages were disclosed in September 2006, Foley immediately resigned and checked himself into rehab. But the Left was not about to be denied a prolonged feeding frenzy, and so reporters and Democrats tried to broaden the scandal to ensnare GOP House leaders. Soon liberals were asking the all-purpose rhetorical question wielded against Republicans since Watergate: "What did they know and when did they know it?" There were calls for the resignation of House Speaker Denny Hastert, who dug in for the fight. Barely able to disguise their glee, journalists speculated hopefully that the scandal would cost Republicans control of Congress. To that end, reporters made sure the story raged for weeks. More than one hundred stories on the Foley scandal were broadcast by ABC, CBS, and NBC in the first week alone, according to a tally by the Media Research Center.

On October 14, 2006, the Associated Press ran one of countless stories about "disgraced former representative Mark Foley." Yet that same day, the same wire service described the late Democratic congressman Gerry Studds of Massachusetts, who had actually engaged in sex with a seventeen-year-old male page, as "a devoted environmentalist and inspiration to the gay community for his openness and push for equal rights." The double standard was nothing short of breathtaking.

Although no one accused Foley of actually engaging in sex with a seventeen-year-old male page, the reprehensible nature of his e-mails and instant messages was enough to end the Republican's career and send the press into paroxysms of righteous indignation. Studds, by contrast—who was censured by the House for having sex with a minor—was rewarded with standing ovations from his constituents, plaudits from the press, five more terms in Congress, and a dignified retirement in 1997. When he died three weeks before the 2006 midterms, the AP went out of its way to quote sympathetic sources like fellow gay Democratic congressman Barney Frank of Massachusetts. According to the AP, Frank said Studds "didn't let the scandal get in his way."

"It was very important to see, for young people in particular, somebody as capable and talented as he be openly gay," said Frank. "That gave a lot people the courage to say, 'I can survive this business in being honest about who I am.'"

The AP also quoted Senator John Kerry lauding Studds as "a committed environmentalist." But in its coverage of Foley that very same day, the AP quoted Kerry as calling the scandal "a Republican cover-up." The Massachusetts Democrat, in the early stages of mounting a second presidential campaign, added disdainfully, "Those from the party that preaches moral values that covered this up have no right to preach moral values anymore."

None of these scandals touched on the White House, and the president was powerless to do anything about them. More importantly, he was powerless to do anything about the media's voracious coverage of the stories.

With so many Republicans ensnared in scandals, Democrats were able to gain traction with their constant charge that the GOP was permeated by a "culture of corruption." But Democrats had their own share of scandals in 2006, even if those scandals were not as eagerly chronicled by the mainstream media. Democratic congresswoman Cynthia McKinney of Georgia punched a Capitol Hill police officer in a fit of pique. FBI agents found $90,000 in suspicious cash in the freezer of Democratic congressman William Jefferson of Louisiana (he would later be charged with bribery). Even Senate Minority Leader Harry Reid collected a million-dollar windfall profit on a shady land deal. But the press paid far less attention to such Democratic scandals, preferring instead to concentrate on the theme of GOP wrongdoing.

Meanwhile, voters were growing weary of the Iraq war, which had been dragging on for more than three years. Americans had grown particularly pessimistic during the months of sectarian warfare following the bombing of the Golden Mosque in Samarra. Fueled in part by the mainstream media's relentlessly negative coverage, there was a growing sense that the president's Iraq policy simply wasn't working. Although Bush was not on the ballot, voters seemed ready to take out their frustrations on at least some congressional Republicans who supported the war.

Liberals smelled blood in the water and pressed their advantage. The left wing of the Democratic Party became increasingly assertive in demanding that candidates vigorously oppose Bush on the war. Most Democrats obliged, although Senator Joe Lieberman, the rare moderate, still refused to abandon his conviction that Bush was doing the right thing in Iraq. For this he paid dearly, as left-wing advocacy groups made good on their threat to recruit an antiwar liberal to challenge Lieberman in the Democratic primary. Lionized by the mainstream media in the months leading up to the August primary, businessman Ned Lamont was able to defeat Lieberman, who nonetheless resolved to run as an independent against Lamont in the general election in November.

It didn't take long for Democrats to utterly disown the man they had nominated for vice president half a dozen years earlier. The day after Lamont's victory, Senate Minority Leader Harry Reid and Senator Chuck Schumer, chairman of the Democratic Senatorial Campaign Committee, kicked Lieberman while he was down.

"Joe Lieberman has been an effective Democratic senator for Connecticut and for America," they allowed in a joint statement. "But the perception was that he was too close to George Bush. And this election was, in many respects, a referendum on the president more than anything else."

The unseemly stampede of Democrats rushing to endorse Lamont included House Minority Leader Nancy Pelosi and every senator even considering a run for president in 2008 — Hillary Rodham Clinton, John Kerry, Evan Bayh, Russ Feingold, and Chris Dodd. Having campaigned for Lieberman right up until the day of the primary, Dodd had no compunction about showing up the next morning at Lamont's jubilant press conference. The eighteen years Dodd and Lieberman had spent together representing the state of Connecticut suddenly meant nothing in the increasingly radicalized Democratic caucus.

"A good friend, a good senator, and a good Democrat," Dodd said of Lieberman before sticking in the shiv. "But now the voters of our party have spoken — and I respect their decision."

Reporters immediately began asking Lieberman if he would step aside, but the old warhorse vowed to press on with his independent campaign. "I am in this race to the end," he told CNN. "For me, it is a cause, and it is a cause not to let this Democratic Party that I joined with the inspiration of President Kennedy in 1960 to be taken over by people who are so far from the mainstream of American life that I fear we will not elect Democrats in the numbers that we should in the future. I'm carrying it on because Lamont really represents polarization and partisanship, which is the last thing we need more of in Washington."

About the only person willing to defend Lieberman was a Republican, Vice President Cheney, who had campaigned against him in the 2000 White House race. Aside from national security, Cheney disagreed with Lieberman on just about everything. And yet the vice president respected Lieberman as the last of a dying breed—a Democrat who held fast to the old-fashioned notion that politics stopped at the water's edge when it came to defending America.

"I'm a big Lieberman fan. I think Joe is a good guy," Cheney told me in his West Wing office. "He was rejected by the Democratic Party in Connecticut, primarily on the issue of the war, and his support for the administration and the president on the war. I thought that was a tragedy, in a sense, because he was the most effective spokesman on the other side for that point of view."

Cheney said he was appalled to see Lieberman "purged" by his own party. "Most of his colleagues in the Senate—in the Democratic caucus in the Senate—campaigned for his opponent and walked away from him," the vice president marveled. "It captured the problem the Democratic Party has—and I do think it's a problem for the party. I think partly it's a problem for the country because, given the nature of this conflict that we're in, it really is important to try to build bipartisan support, as we did during the Cold War."

Cheney lamented the lack of such bipartisan support for the war against terrorism, which replaced Communism as the dominant global threat after the Cold War. "Seems to be impossible to put it together," he told me. "The other side is bound and determined to do whatever they can to try to defeat the president on this issue."

Cheney was equally blunt on the campaign trail, where he stumped for Republicans by warning against a Democratic takeover of Congress. "As we make our case to the voters in this election year, it's vital to keep issues of national security at the top of our agenda," he exhorted an audience of Republicans in Phoenix. "The president and I welcome the discussion, because every voter in America needs to know where we stand, as well as how the leaders of the Democratic Party view the war on terror. Their floor leader in the Senate, Harry Reid, boasted publicly of his efforts to kill the PATRIOT Act. The chairman of the Democratic Party, Howard Dean, said the capture of Saddam Hussein would not make America any safer. And now Mr. Dean's party has turned its back on Senator Joe Lieberman."

Cheney hailed Lieberman as "one of the most loyal and distinguished Democrats of his generation."

"Joe is also an unapologetic supporter of the fight against terror," the vice president said in Phoenix. "He voted to support military action in Iraq when most other senators in both parties did the same—and he's had the courage to stick by that vote even when things get tough. And now, for that reason alone, the Dean Democrats have defeated Joe Lieberman. Their choice, instead, is a candidate whose explicit goal is to give up the fight against the terrorists in Iraq. Never mind that Iraq is a fellow democracy. Never mind that the Iraqi people and their elected leaders are counting on us. What these Democrats are pushing now is the very kind of retreat that has been tried in the past. It is contrary to our values, it would betray our friends, and it would only heighten the danger to the United States. So the choice before the American people is becoming clearer every day. For the sake of our security, this nation must reject any strategy of resignation and defeatism in the face of determined enemies.

"We have to face the simple truth," Cheney concluded. "The enemies that struck America are weakened and fractured, but they are still
lethal and still desperately trying to hit us again. We have a duty to act
against them as swiftly and effectively as we possibly can. Either we are
serious about fighting this war or we are not. And with George W. Bush
leading this nation, we are serious, and we will not let down our guard."

But neither Bush nor Cheney was on the ballot this time around.
That made it difficult for chief White House strategist Karl Rove and
Republican National Committee chairman Ken Mehlman to rally
Republicans around a central, unifying theme the way they had in
2004. The two men had trouble enforcing discipline on hundreds of
disparate GOP candidates, some of whom seemed alarmingly com-
placent. Six-term Indiana congressman John Hostettler didn't bother
raising much money or making many campaign appearances. When
he finally ran a TV ad, it was to brag that he was one of a handful of
Republicans to have voted against the Iraq war resolution of 2002.
The national Republican Party spent $1 million on airtime for
Hostettler, but it was difficult to help a candidate who did not seem
interested in helping himself.

Other Republicans actually refused assistance from the national
party, thinking they would score points for appearing independent in
a tough political environment for the GOP. Fifteen-term congressman Jim Leach of Iowa, who had also voted against the Iraq war, actually threatened to caucus with the Democrats if the RNC continued
to criticize Leach's Democratic opponent in campaign mailings. Similarly, three-term congresswoman Melissa Hart of Pennsylvania asked
the RNC to stop criticizing her Democratic opponent, who had no
compunction about going negative on Hart. Determined to occupy
the higher ground, the Republican refused to return fire.

To be sure, there were plenty of Republicans who gratefully made
use of the administration's considerable political expertise. But others ignored White House pleas to campaign more aggressively.

"I'd be running on the economy and I'd be running on national security—but since I'm not running, I can only serve as an adviser to those who are," Bush said at a press conference. "I'd say, look at what the economy has done. It's strong. We created a lot of jobs," he suggested. "I'd be telling people that the Democrats will raise your taxes."

But most of all, Bush wanted to reprise his electoral strategy of 2002 and 2004, when the GOP won on national security in general and Iraq in particular. If only more Republicans this time around were willing to fearlessly defend the war, in stark contrast to the Democrats.

"What matters is that in this campaign that we clarify the different point of view," the president said. "And there are a lot of people in the Democratic Party who believe that the best course of action is to leave Iraq before the job is done. Period. And they're wrong. And the American people have got to understand the consequence of leaving Iraq before the job is done. We're not going to leave Iraq before the job is done," he repeated for emphasis. "We'll complete the mission in Iraq. I can't tell you exactly when it's going to be done. But I do know that it's important for us to support the Iraqi people, who have shown incredible courage in their desire to live in a free society. And if we ever give up the desire to help people who live in freedom, we will have lost our soul as a nation, as far as I'm concerned."

Bush warned that if Democrats were to win control of Congress, they might try to "cut off money" for the Iraq mission in order "to get our troops out." It was the first time the president had publicly raised the possibility that Congress would use its power of the purse to thwart his Iraq policy. And yet he made clear that even if such a scenario were to materialize, he would never give in to Democratic demands for a withdrawal.

"We're not leaving, so long as I'm the president," he vowed unequivocally. "That would be a huge mistake. It would send an unbelievably terrible signal to reformers across the region. It would say we've abandoned our desire to change the conditions that create terror. It would give the terrorists a safe haven from which to launch attacks. It would embolden Iran. It would embolden extremists. No, we're not leaving."

Although Bush didn't come right out and say it, he strongly implied that Democrats were giving aid and comfort to the enemy through their campaign rhetoric about withdrawal. "Any sign that says we're going to leave before the job is done simply emboldens terrorists, and creates a certain amount of doubt for people so they won't take the risk necessary to help a civil society evolve in the country," he said. "I'm sure they're watching the campaign carefully."

Furthermore, the president warned that if the U.S. were to "concede territory to the terrorists," the difficulties in Iraq would merely multiply and spill across the broader Middle East. "If you think it's bad now, imagine what Iraq would look like if the United States leaves before this government can defend itself and sustain itself," he said. "Chaos in Iraq would be very unsettling in the region."

But there was already a fair amount of chaos in Iraq, which was taking its toll on both Bush and the public. "Sometimes I'm frustrated," he conceded. "War is not a time of joy. These aren't joyous times. These are challenging times, and they're difficult times, and they're straining the psyche of our country. I understand that. You know, nobody likes to see innocent people die. Nobody wants to turn on their TV on a daily basis and see havoc wrought by terrorists."

Toward the end of his press conference, the president called on reporter Ken Herman of Cox Newspapers, who had been covering Bush since he was governor of Texas.

"Mr. President, polls continue to show sagging support for the war in Iraq," Herman said. "Is it your belief that long-term results will vindicate your strategy and people will change their mind about it? Or is this the kind of thing you're doing because you think it's right and you don't care if you ever gain public support for it?"

"You've now been covering me for quite a while, twelve years," Bush reminded Herman. "I don't think you've ever heard me say, 'Gosh, I'd better change positions because the polls say this or that.' I've been here long enough to understand you cannot make good decisions if you're trying to chase a poll."

Thus, while Bush cared deeply about public support for his Iraq policy, he was not about to jettison his convictions when that support began to erode. "Look, I'm going to do what I think is right, and if people don't like me for it, that's just the way it is," the president concluded.

Such was the stoicism of George W. Bush as he headed into the home stretch of the 2006 midterm campaign. He gamely tried to shore up support for his Iraq policy by giving a series of five high-profile speeches aimed at explaining the imperative of victory. He sought to counter the daily onslaught of negative news from Iraq by scoring daily victories, such as the arrest of an al-Zarqawi deputy who had supervised the bombers of the Golden Mosque in Samarra. He tried to play a constructive role in ending weeks of summer warfare that erupted between Israel and Hezbollah forces in Lebanon. He kept predicting that while Republicans would almost certainly lose seats in both the House and Senate, they would ultimately retain majorities in both chambers.

And yet privately, a grim reality was setting in at the White House. While Bush never abandoned his commitment to stabilize Iraq, he gradually came to realize such a goal could not be accomplished without a fundamental change of course. Defense Secretary Donald Rumsfeld sensed it as well, even as he realized he might not be the best person to implement such a change. The pugnacious seventy-four-year-old was well aware of his own status as a lightning rod for criticism of the administration's Iraq policy. Not wishing to be an albatross around the president's neck, Rumsfeld had twice offered his resignation to Bush during the height of the Abu Ghraib prisoner abuse scandal back in 2004. Both times, the president had rejected the offers and urged Rumsfeld to stay on.

But now the old warrior was approaching another crossroads—the very real possibility that whatever change in Iraq policy Bush was contemplating would coincide with a change of power in Congress. If Democrats took the House and Senate, Rumsfeld could count on spending the last two years of the Bush administration answering hostile questions on Capitol Hill. And even if Republicans managed to hang on to the reins of power in Congress, Rumsfeld worried that his utility to the president would continue to diminish. During a series of conversations at the White House, Bush quietly asked Rumsfeld to begin a Pentagon review aimed at finding a better way forward in Iraq. Rumsfeld agreed on the need for such a change, saying the effort to stabilize Iraq was not proceeding "well enough or fast enough." He ventured that the president "may need fresh eyes" on the process, a subtle way of suggesting he was willing to step aside. Bush took note of the overture, but said nothing at the time. However, during subsequent meetings at the White House, Bush warmed to the idea that it would be best for Rumsfeld to step down after the election, regardless of which party won. Rumsfeld graciously agreed.

"He was sort of the ultimate realist," a senior administration official told me. "He's a guy who has the capacity, I think, to stand back and be objective about the set of circumstances he finds himself in and not personalize it, which is a hard thing for a lot of people to do. And he had made it clear that if it ever got to the point where he was more of a problem than part of the solution, that he was perfectly prepared to step aside. And that's what he and the president worked out."

But Bush did not want the change announced before the election because he knew it would be interpreted as a desperate political ploy to preserve Republican control of Congress. Besides, he had not yet secured Rumsfeld's likely replacement, Robert Gates, who had served as CIA director during his father's presidency.

But five days before the election, a reporter asked Bush whether he planned to keep Rumsfeld and Cheney on for the rest of his administration. He knew that if he disclosed his plan to replace Rumsfeld, troops in the field would view it as Bush cravenly throwing a loyalist under the bus to score cheap political points. On the other hand, if the president deceived the reporter, he knew he would be excoriated after the election. Bush decided to throw himself on this political grenade and let it explode later.

"Yes," the president prevaricated. "Both those men are doing fantastic jobs and I strongly support them."

But by now even most Republicans were privately acknowledging they would almost certainly lose control of the House. Many also fretted they would lose up to five Senate seats, dropping from a fifty-five-seat majority to a fifty-seat tie with the Democratic caucus. Vice President Cheney, in his tie-breaking role as president of the Senate, would be the only thing preventing a full Democratic takeover of Congress.

Democrats were so confident of winning the keys to the leadership offices on Capitol Hill that they were practically measuring for drapes. Asked which offices she would commandeer if she were to become Speaker, House Minority Leader Nancy Pelosi replied with a laugh, "I'll have any suite I want!"

Republicans were reduced to praying for a miracle, or at the very least an eleventh-hour Democratic controversy that might save the GOP. Some believed their prayers had been answered when Senator John Kerry made a gaffe of colossal proportions just days before the election.

Speaking to a group of college students in California, Kerry said, "You know, education, if you make the most of it, you study hard, you do your homework and you make an effort to be smart, you can do well. And if you don't, you get stuck in Iraq."

Amazingly, the man whose 2004 presidential campaign was hamstrung by his decades-old denunciation of fellow Vietnam veterans as "war criminals" was now insulting the intelligence of U.S. soldiers and Marines bravely serving in Iraq. As commander in chief, Bush felt compelled to publicly defend his troops the next day.

"The senator's suggestion that the men and women of our military are somehow uneducated is insulting and it is shameful," he told a raucous crowd in Georgia. "The members of the United States military are plenty smart, and they are plenty brave, and the senator from Massachusetts owes them an apology."

But Kerry refused, saying he had been trying to make a joke about Bush, not insult the troops. "Let me make it crystal clear, as crystal clear as I know how: I apologize to no one for my criticism of the president and of his broken policy," he said at a news conference shortly after Bush's demand. "If anyone owes our troops in the fields an apology, it is the president and his failed team and a Republican majority in the Congress that has been willing to stamp—rubber-stamp—policies that have done injury to our troops and to their families. My statement yesterday—and the White House knows this full well—was a botched joke about the president and the president's people, not about the troops," he added. "The White House's attempt to distort my true statement is a remarkable testament to their abject failure in making America safe."

If the insult in question had been hurled by a conservative Republican, the mainstream media would have dismissed the "botched joke" excuse as absurd and proceeded to crucify the offender. But since the remark had been hurled by a liberal Democrat, the mainstream media tried to lend credence to the "botched joke" excuse and even portray Kerry as the victim.

"What happened today is an object lesson in how, in this day and age, an idle political remark gets seized upon, becomes fodder for the talk shows, the blogs, and the politicians, and suddenly obscures discussion of all other issues," complained Charlie Gibson on ABC.

Turning to self-described liberal Democrat George Stephanopoulos, Gibson suggested Bush was the villain for taking offense at Kerry's remark. "George, does anyone at the White House really think that Senator Kerry was in some way denigrating the intelligence of American troops?" asked Gibson with exaggerated incredulity.

"Not exactly," replied Stephanopoulus, whose transformation from President Clinton's spokesman to ABC anchorman still disgusted even arch-liberal Helen Thomas. "But they don't think it's their job to give John Kerry the benefit of the doubt."

The next morning, the *New York Times* reported on its front page that President Bush had "attacked Senator Kerry of Massachusetts over the war in Iraq." Readers had to slog all the way to the fifteenth paragraph of the story, which continued on page eighteen, to read what Kerry had said about the troops. The *Washington Post* made no mention of the story on its own front page, a piece of journalistic real estate reserved for the likes of "macaca" stories.

But the rest of America was not buying this lame spin from Kerry and his apologists in the mainstream media. Even radio "shock jock" Don Imus, who admitted to voting for Kerry in the 2004 presidential election, now beseeched him to end a controversy that might cost Democrats the midterms.

"Please stop it," Imus told Kerry on his radio and TV show two days after the insult. "Stop talking. Go home, get on the bike, go windsurfing, anything. Stop it. You're going to ruin this."

Kerry explained he was canceling all further campaign appearances for fellow Democrats, who had banned him anyway after his insult of the troops. "I'm coming back to Washington today so that

I'm not a distraction, because I don't want to be a distraction to these campaigns," Kerry said. "I'm not going to go to some place that a Congressman's going to get embroiled in this, because I want them to win."

Amazingly, Kerry was still refusing to apologize. "The people who owe an apology are people like Donald Rumsfeld, who didn't send enough troops, who didn't listen to the generals, who has made every mistake in the book," Kerry fumed. "Frankly, the media needs to stand up to them, too. They shouldn't be allowed to do that. This is Swift Boat stuff all over again."

"God, just stop it, I'm begging you," Imus said. "I love you, but just stop it. I'm begging you."

Even fellow Democratic senator Hillary Rodham Clinton, while making a campaign appearance at a Veterans of Foreign Wars post, felt compelled to call Kerry's remarks "inappropriate." Democratic congressman Harold Ford of Tennessee added, "Kerry was wrong to say what he said. He needs to apologize to our troops."

Bush agreed. "It didn't sound like a joke to me," he said. "Anybody who is in a position to serve this country ought to understand the consequences of words, and our troops deserve the full support of people in government."

Vice President Cheney weighed in on the controversy during a campaign speech in Idaho. "You all remember John Kerry—the senator who voted for the $87 billion before he voted against it, the guy that was always lecturing us about 'nuance,'" Cheney deadpanned, drawing laughter from the audience. "He's the one, you'll recall, who last year said that American soldiers were terrorizing children in Iraq. And just this week he took another swipe at the U.S. military."

The crowd booed as Cheney recited Kerry's insult.

"Senator Kerry said he was just making a joke, and he botched it up," Cheney added. "I guess we didn't get the nuance. Actually, he was for the joke before he was against it."

The final blow came from a Minnesota National Guard unit stationed in Iraq. The unit released a photo of eight U.S. soldiers holding a large white banner with blue letters that spelled out a mocking reply to Kerry's insult: "HALP US JON CARRY—WE R STUCK HEAR N IRAK."

One day after vowing he would "apologize to no one," Kerry reversed course and issued a written apology: "I sincerely regret that my words were misinterpreted to wrongly imply anything negative about those in uniform and I personally apologize to any service member, family member, or American who was offended."

Kerry's capitulation incensed the mainstream media, which had gone to bat for him by trying to downplay the controversy. On NBC's *Today* show, host Matt Lauer was still trying to breathe life into the discredited "botched joke" excuse.

"He made a joke!" Lauer argued to Bush's former chief of staff, Andy Card. "He says he blew the joke and inadvertently sounded as though he questioned the intelligence of U.S. troops in Iraq. Look me in the eye and tell me if, with even a fraction of your heart, you think John Kerry meant to question the intelligence of U.S. troops in Iraq."

When Card pointed out that much of the criticism of Kerry had come from fellow Democrats, Lauer left no doubt about his own sympathies. "I think a lot of Democrats should have shame on their shoulders, because they ran away from this guy as opposed to standing up and saying it was just a mistake," he railed.

Such was the mainstream media's double standard as the midterm campaign came to a close. John Kerry insulted the intelligence of American troops, and the press portrayed him as a victim. George Allen uttered the word *macaca* and the press savaged him as a remorseless racist.

Truth be told, neither Kerry nor Allen helped their 2008 presidential ambitions with their ill-advised remarks. But Allen, not Kerry, was on the ballot in 2006. And the beleaguered Republican who was supposed to coast to reelection in the Senate now found himself unable to even contemplate a bid for the White House.

"Pay attention to the task at hand," Allen told me when I asked about his plans for 2008. "I'll be happy to be alive at the end of this election."

Chapter Eight

"Bush Makes Me Sick"

D AN RATHER WAS SO DEPRESSED that he went alone to a movie
theater to watch the film *Good Night, and Good Luck*—for the
fifth time. The disgraced CBS newsman took comfort in watching
and rewatching George Clooney's liberal homage to Edward R.
Murrow. The simplistic, black-and-white morality play always ended
the same way—with Murrow, the intrepid CBS crusader, bringing
down Senator Joseph McCarthy, the evil anti-Communist. If only
Rather's crusade against President Bush had ended the same way.
Instead, the documents he had trumpeted to savage Bush's military
record turned out to be bogus. And the only career Rather destroyed
was his own.

For Rather, the end had come slowly, in a series of gradual humil-
iations spanning an excruciating two years. It was a far cry from the
sudden downfall of his star producer, Mary Mapes, who, in her own
words, was "spectacularly, publicly, embarrassingly fired" in the
immediate aftermath of the scandal known as "Memogate." CBS also

forced out senior vice president Betsy West, as well as top producers Josh Howard and Mary Murphy. For a while it appeared as though CBS News president Andrew Heyward would hang on to his job, but he was eventually drummed out by CBS chairman Leslie Moonves. That left only Rather, the newsman at the center of the storm, still employed by the vaunted "Tiffany" network.

Actually, "employed" was a bit of a stretch, at least toward the end. After being forced from his anchor chair at the CBS *Evening News* a year before his planned retirement, Rather was allowed to continue working at *60 Minutes II*. But the program was canceled a year after Memogate, forcing CBS to shuffle Rather over to the original *60 Minutes* show. Even there, Rather received only a fraction of the assignments given to other reporters. Eventually, the work dried up altogether. For months, the legendary newsman with the $12 million salary was given nothing to do. When it came time to renew his contract, which was scheduled to expire in November 2006, CBS offered the seventy-four-year-old only an office, a secretary, and permanent banishment from the airwaves of the network that had employed him for forty-four years. It was downright humiliating.

"My departure before the term of my contract represents CBS's final acknowledgment, after a protracted struggle, that they had not lived up to their obligation to allow me to do substantive work there," Rather said in a bitter statement. "As for their offers of a future with only an office but no assignments, it just isn't in me to sit around doing nothing."

But nothing was all CBS would offer.

"There was no bigger role for him to play anymore," Moonves said. "I'm sorry it ended the way it did."

Tonight Show host Jay Leno could not resist a parting shot. "Today was Dan Rather's last day at CBS," the comedian reported. "He turned in his letter of resignation, which later turned out to be a forgery."

Such would be the enduring legacy of Dan Rather, whose igno-minious professional demise was the direct result of his blind deter-mination to destroy the presidency of George W. Bush. But the fact that Rather was actually held to account for his liberal bias made him a rarity among reporters, most of whom recklessly savaged the Bush administration with impunity. Over time, this unrelenting crit-icism succeeded in turning the public against the president, whose effectiveness in prosecuting the war on terror was eroded accord-ingly. It was a vicious cycle in which the press actively tore Bush down and then feigned detachment as they "reported" on his dimin-ished potency.

To that end, the mainstream media spent three years openly root-ing for an indictment of White House political strategist Karl Rove. Journalists hinted darkly that Rove was the culprit who diabolically leaked the name of CIA employee Valerie Plame in order to punish her husband, Joseph Wilson, an outspoken Bush critic. Rove was pil-loried even after his lawyer announced that special counsel Patrick Fitzgerald had assured him Rove was not a target of the investigation.

"But this isn't just about the Facts," *Newsweek* harrumphed. "It's about what Rove's foes regard as a higher Truth: that he is a one-man epicenter of a narrative of Evil."

Those foes included *Newsweek* itself, not to mention the rest of the mainstream media, which indeed considered Rove's aggressive advocacy of Bush's conservatism nothing less than evil.

So the press was crestfallen when it learned Plame's identity had been disclosed not by Rove, but by a politically moderate member of the Bush administration, deputy secretary of state Richard Armitage. Reporters were sympathetic toward Armitage because he was aligned with former secretary of state Colin Powell, widely portrayed as the lone voice of reason in an administration of warmongering neocons. Thus, when Armitage said he meant no harm by disclosing Plame's identity, the press accepted his explanation at face value, buried the story, and moved on. The double standard in media coverage of Armitage and Rove was so blatant that it outraged even liberal columnist David Broder of the *Washington Post*. Broder opined that publications such as *Newsweek* "owe Karl Rove an apology." That plea, unsurprisingly, fell on deaf ears.

With Rove cleared by the prosecutor, reporters had to content themselves with obsessing over Lewis "Scooter" Libby, Cheney's former chief of staff, who was indicted for lying to investigators. In political terms, Libby was a relatively small fish; the vast majority of the American public had never heard of him before he was indicted. But with Rove off the hook, Libby was the highest-ranking Bush administration official charged with a crime, and so the press tried to inflate his importance. Never mind that he was not charged with the underlying crime of leaking Plame's name. Oceans of ink and eons of airtime were devoted to puffing up the significance of an obscure, behind-the-scenes apparatchik named Scooter.

By contrast, reporters downplayed the significance of liberal Democrat Sandy Berger, who had served as national security adviser to President Clinton, stealing highly classified documents from the National Archives. The documents were critical of the Clinton administration's anti-terrorism efforts at the turn of the millennium. Berger's access to these files in the Archives gave him a chance to scrub the historical record in advance of the 9-11 Commission hearings in 2003. The theft was not publicly disclosed until a year later, when Berger was a foreign policy adviser to presidential candidate John Kerry. Berger, who was on the short list to become secretary of state in the event of a Kerry victory, shrugged off the episode as "an honest mistake." "I inadvertently took a few documents from the archives," he told reporters. "I deeply regret the sloppiness involved."

Clinton vouched for this explanation and laughingly recalled the disorganized Berger as chronically "buried beneath papers" in his West Wing office. He dismissed the flap as a "non-story" and suggested it had been "leaked" by Republicans to divert attention from the 9-11 Commission's criticism of the Bush administration. Incredibly, the press parroted Clinton's spin, turning what should have been a major scandal about a Democratic theft of classified documents into an utterly unsubstantiated fantasy about Republican "dirty tricks." Reporters credulously portrayed Berger as a lovable "absent-minded professor" type incapable of intentionally breaking the law. They even ridiculed reports that Berger had actually hidden some documents in his socks.

Only after the 2004 presidential election was safely over did Berger admit that his removal of the highly classified documents had indeed been intentional. Furthermore, he admitted to spiriting the papers away to his office and cutting them up with scissors. So much for Berger's "honest mistake." At his sentencing in September 2005, he was fined $50,000, placed on probation, and stripped of his security clearance for three years. But even then reporters pooh-poohed the story, insisting Berger could not have caused any harm because he admitted stealing only copies of classified documents, not originals. The press refused to entertain the possibility that Berger, now a proven liar, might also have lied to investigators about how much he stole. Such skepticism would have come naturally to journalists if the thief in question had been a conservative Republican. But Berger was a liberal Democrat, and so the press accepted at face value his claim to have stolen only those documents Archives officials had actually caught him stealing.

The press continued to downplay the story in late 2006, when the National Archives inspector general released a damning report with explosive new details about Berger's thievery. For starters, the much-maligned account of Berger stuffing documents in his socks turned out to be true. Berger had been caught in the act after excusing himself from the document examination room for one of his innumerable "bathroom breaks."

"He walked out the door and into the hallway," reported Archives employee John Laster. "He was stooped over right outside the doorway. He was fiddling with something white, which looked to be a piece of paper or multiple pieces of paper. It appeared to be rolled around his ankle and underneath his pant leg, with a portion of the paper sticking out underneath." In case anyone missed the point, Laster added, "There was clearly something there more than his pants and socks."

Incredibly, the press discounted this eyewitness report and lent credence to Berger's lame explanation that "his shoes frequently come untied and his socks frequently fall down." It was the absent-minded professor defense all over again.

A month after the sock episode, according to the inspector general's report, Berger returned to the Archives and pulled an even more brazen caper. After stuffing his pockets with highly classified terrorism documents and equally sensitive notes, he waited until guards left for the evening so he could slip away without being searched.

"Mr. Berger exited the Archives on to Pennsylvania Avenue, the north entrance. It was dark," the report said. "He headed towards a construction area on Ninth Street. Mr. Berger looked up and down the street, up into the windows of the Archives and the DOJ [Department of Justice], and did not see anyone. He removed the documents from his pockets, folded the notes into a 'V' shape and inserted the documents in the center. He walked inside the construction fence and slid the documents under a trailer."

Having completed this dead-drop espionage, Berger later returned to the scene of the crime to furtively retrieve his ill-gotten booty. Two days later, he was informed by Archive employees that his removal of documents had been detected.

"Berger panicked because he realized he was caught," said the inspector general's report, which recounted the thief's instinctive reaction. "Berger lied."

Eventually, after realizing his denials were fruitless, Berger grudgingly admitted taking the documents—but only those that Archives employees had noticed were missing. "I realized I was giving a benign explanation for what was not benign," he conceded.

He insisted he had taken them only for his own convenience, not to sanitize the Clinton administration's historical record on terrorism. And yet on one occasion, Berger knowingly stole two copies of the same document, which blew a major hole through his "convenience" defense.

Fewer than three weeks after the inspector general's report was released, the House Committee on Oversight and Government Reform detonated an entirely new series of Berger bombshells. In a detailed report, the committee revealed that Berger had been allowed to root unsupervised through classified files of original, uncopied, uninventoried documents on terrorism. Several Archives officials acknowledged Berger could have pilfered to his heart's delight and they "would never know what, if any, original documents were missing." The report painted the most vivid account to date of Berger aggressively breaking the rules at the Archives in order to be left alone with highly classified documents. These stunning revelations were buried on page A-4 of the *Washington Post*. The *New York Times*, which bragged daily of publishing "all the news that's fit to print," didn't print a word.

The *Times* did, however, manage to find room for a 3,500-word story that gratuitously exposed another top-secret weapon in the Bush administration's arsenal against terrorism. Run by the CIA and Treasury Department, the perfectly legal and highly effective program traced the financial transactions of terrorists and had led directly to the capture of several major al Qaeda figures. The Bush administration begged the *Times* not to disclose the program for fear of losing yet another advantage against the bad guys. But the *Times* had no interest in helping the White House preserve national security.

"The disclosure of this program is disgraceful," Bush fumed to reporters. "We're at war with a bunch of people who want to hurt the United States of America, and for people to leak that program, and for a newspaper to publish it, does great harm to the United States of America."

Having been pilloried for failing to "connect the dots" before September 11, Bush was once again being pilloried for connecting them afterward. "The 9-11 Commission recommended that the government be robust in tracing money," he said. "If you want to figure out what the terrorists are doing, you try to follow their money. And that's exactly what we're doing. And the fact that a newspaper disclosed it makes it harder to win this war on terror."

White House press secretary Tony Snow was even more blunt. "The *New York Times* and other news organizations ought to think long and hard about whether a public's right to know, in some cases, might override somebody's right to live," he told reporters. "And whether, in fact, the publications of these could place in jeopardy the safety of fellow Americans."

One reporter told Snow the banking records story was "parallel" to the terrorist surveillance program, "which gives the perception, if nothing else, that it's an arrogance of presidential power." But Snow would not allow the reporter to get away with such bias.

"What you've done is just reveal the lens through which you're looking at it, which is suspicious, skeptical, and doesn't seem to understand that the word 'terrorist' has real meaning," said Snow, adding that even the *Times* story did "not convey the dark impression you try to convey in the question."

Vice President Cheney credited the programs to track financing and intercept communications with helping prevent a terrorist attack on America for five long years. "The *New York Times* has now made it more difficult for us to prevent attacks in the future," he railed. "Publishing this highly classified information about our sources and methods for collecting intelligence will enable the terrorists to look for ways to defeat our efforts. These kinds of stories also adversely affect our relationships with people who work with us against the terrorists. In the future, they will be less likely to cooperate if they think the United States is incapable of keeping a secret."

Cheney was further outraged by the Pulitzer Prizes awarded to the *Times* for exposing the terrorist surveillance program and the *Washington Post* for exposing the CIA overseas prisons. "What is doubly disturbing for me is that not only have they gone forward with these stories, but they've been rewarded for it," he marveled.

The public backlash against the *New York Times* was swift and furious. "It's a terrorist tip sheet," said radio talk-show host Scott Hennen. "That's basically what the *New York Times* has become, hasn't it?"

Times executive editor Bill Keller wrote a letter complaining about the "angry words of conservative bloggers and TV or radio pundits who say that drawing attention to the government's anti-terror measures is unpatriotic and dangerous. (I could ask, if that's the case, why they are drawing so much attention to the story themselves by yelling about it on the airwaves and the Internet.)"

Keller, who had once accused Bush of "public piety," now piously defended his decision to print the banking story. "It's an unusual and powerful thing, this freedom that our founders gave to the press," he sermonized. "The people who invented this country saw an aggressive, independent press as a protective measure against the abuse of power in a democracy." Laughably, Keller denied "any animus toward the current administration" and shrugged off his paper's inability to find anything abusive or illegal about the banking program. "It's not our job to pass judgment on whether this program is legal or effective," he wrote.

"Well, it is your job to exercise editorial judgment," countered Snow, who had been a journalist for twenty-seven years. "You simply cannot say, 'We got this story, we're going to publish it, but we don't have to worry about whether it's legal or effective.'"

Besides, its effectiveness was not in doubt. The program had helped authorities apprehend the mastermind of a terrorist bombing in Bali and a terror financier in Brooklyn. It had also helped break up several terror cells and helped police track suspects in the London subway bombings.

"With that kind of demonstrated efficacy, the question is why on earth make the editorial decision that this program no longer should be effective by exposing it?" Snow asked.

Keller wasn't the only journalist making dubious editorial decisions about coverage of the war on terror. CNN actually decided to broadcast footage of U.S. troops in Iraq being shot by snipers who videotaped their own atrocities. The public was outraged by the move, and one hotel chain even removed CNN from TV sets in its rooms.

"What is CNN doing running terrorist tape of terrorist shooting Americans?" demanded Lynne Cheney during an appearance on the network. "Do you want us to win?"

"The answer, of course, is we want the United States to win," anchorman Wolf Blitzer replied. "We are Americans. There's no doubt about it. You think we want terrorists to win?"

"Then why are you running terrorist propaganda?"

"With all due respect," Blitzer said, "this is not terrorist propaganda."

"Oh, Wolf!"

"This is reporting the news, which is what we do," Blitzer insisted. "We're not partisan."

"Where did you get the film?"

"We got the film—look, this is an issue that has been widely discussed," said Blitzer, opting not to mention that CNN had gotten the film from a terrorist group. "This is an issue that we reported on extensively. We make no apologies for showing that. That was a very carefully considered decision why we did that. And I think that if you're—"

"Well, I think it's shocking."

"—if you're a serious journalist, you want to report the news. Sometimes the news is good, sometimes the news isn't so good."

"But Wolf, there's a difference between news and terrorist propaganda," Mrs. Cheney pointed out. "Why are you giving the terrorists a forum?"

"And if you put it in context, that's what news is," Blitzer said. "We said it was propaganda."

So much for his assertion, moments earlier, that "this is not terrorist propaganda."

The sad truth was that Terry Moran had been right when he had admitted back in 2005 that the mainstream media had a "deep, anti-military bias." While most journalists weren't that honest about it, every once in a while the mask slipped, and America caught a glimpse of the media's unvarnished contempt for the brave men and women who volunteered to serve in the armed forces.

"I don't support our troops," *Los Angeles Times* columnist Joel Stein declared in a shocking screed. "When you volunteer for the U.S. military," he raged, "you're willingly signing up to be a fighting tool of American imperialism." Stein, who bragged that he "grew up with money, did well in school, and hasn't so much as served on jury duty for his country," chastised fellow liberals for exempting troops from their criticism of the war.

"Blaming the president is a little too easy," he wrote. "The truth is that people who pull triggers are ultimately responsible, whether they're following orders or not. An army of people making individual moral choices may be inefficient, but an army of people ignoring their morality is horrifying."

As an opinion columnist, Stein's smear against the military could be chalked up to freedom of expression. But ostensibly objective journalists overwhelmingly shared Stein's antipathy toward the military in general and Bush in particular.

"Bush makes me sick," wrote John Green, executive producer of ABC's *Good Morning America*, in an e-mail obtained by the Drudge Report. "I'm going to puke."

The daily tsunami of relentlessly anti-Bush coverage prompted me to ask the president whether he thought the mainstream media had a liberal bias.

"There are a lot of studies that show that most of the people who actually write or report the news would not support me for president, I'll put it to you that way," Bush told me.

Nor did these mainstream media journalists support the Iraq war, judging from their overwhelmingly negative coverage. Fortunately, a burgeoning alternative media was providing a more balanced account of the conflict. So were the soldiers and Marines themselves, who were chronicling their progress in clear-eyed letters and computer messages from the field.

"There's a lot of bloggers and a lot of kids writing back to their families," Bush told me. "I sometimes get a different picture from what the average person sees on the news." He added, "I get complaints from people that say, 'Gosh, I'm getting a different story from Iraq than that which I see on the news.'"

Such complaints fell on deaf ears in the mainstream media. On CBS, liberal editor Brian Montopoli asked liberal correspondent Allen Pizzey "whether the media is reporting the war through an anti-administration, liberal-bias lens."

"I dismiss that," Pizzey scoffed. "The Bush administration in particular thinks that anything that doesn't wholly support everything they say is against them." He said journalists had an obligation to expose Bush's lies about Iraq. "If the administration makes idiotic claims, or claims that are patently, to us on the ground, wrong, why should we not report that they're wrong?" he railed. "Now, no reporter is as objective as we'd like to be. Objectivity is a principle to which we strive to adhere, but we all have our own little biases—our upbringing, our personal political beliefs, whatever touches us in a human way. All of that affects our reporting. But I don't think that we have a particular administration bias. I don't care one way or another. I'm not even American," he snorted. (He was born in Canada.) "I just happen to work for Americans. I just do my job."

Such were the attitudes of journalists who chronicled the presidency of George W. Bush. No wonder he was in trouble.

Chapter Nine

"Can't Win 'Em All"

George Allen began his speech by tossing out a football to someone in the audience. But instead of falling back on his usual gridiron metaphors, he opted to compare himself to a tree that had been battered by a gale.

"My friends, sometimes winds, political or otherwise, can blow the leaves off branches and even break limbs," said Allen, flanked by his bravely smiling wife and the leather-faced senior senator from Virginia, John Warner. "But a deep-rooted tree will stand, stay standing. It will regrow in the next season."

This was evidently meant to suggest Allen still intended to be the Republican nominee for president when voters went to the polls in exactly two years. Fat chance. The man who would forever be linked to the word *macaca* had just lost his Senate seat in a race that was never supposed to be competitive. Allen, who had led Democrat Jim Webb by double-digit margins in pre-macaca polling, managed to garner just 49.25 percent of the vote. Webb had squeaked to victory with 49.55 percent. Since the margin of victory was less than half a percentage point, Allen was entitled to a recount at taxpayer expense. But after two days of eyeballing the numbers, he concluded the results would probably not be changed by protracted litigation that he said "could drag on all the way until Christmas."

"The Bible teaches us that there's a time and place for everything," Allen said. "And today, I have called and congratulated Jim Webb and his team for their victory. They had the prevailing winds."

Allen was not merely conceding a single congressional contest. As the last of six Republican senators to throw in the towel in the 2006 midterms, Allen was handing Democrats in effect a 51–49 majority in the upper chamber (officially, only forty-nine senators were Democrats, but both independents—Connecticut's Joe Lieberman and Vermont's Bernie Sanders—would caucus with Democrats). Since Democrats had already won control of the House on election night, Allen's Senate concession officially swung control of the entire Congress to Democrats for the first time in a dozen years. The shift would have fateful consequences for the final two years of the Bush presidency.

A Democratic Congress would test the president in ways he hadn't been tested before. Divided control of government would call for compromise—not always the most natural thing for a president so wedded to his own convictions. This was uncharted terrain for the White House, which had been three-for-three in elections—winning the presidency in 2000, gaining the Senate in 2002, and expanding congressional majorities and winning reelection in 2004.

"Can't win 'em all," Vice President Cheney told me with a rueful smile in his West Wing office. "We'd run out our string. It had been twelve years since we'd taken the Congress, and I think that there's some truth to the notion that the Republicans had gotten used to being in the majority and took it for granted." Cheney did not try to sugarcoat the reasons for the GOP's defeat. "You had this perception,

I think, among some of our Republican supporters that the Congress had gotten profligate in spending and had lost its way," he said.

For example, congressional Republicans had tried to soak taxpayers for $320 million to build a bridge to an Alaskan airport serving a small town of fewer than nine thousand. The "bridge to nowhere" came to symbolize a Republican Party that was "untethered from its roots in fiscal conservatism," White House chief of staff Josh Bolten told me. Although Bush constantly railed against earmarks, their significance was downplayed by Bolten, who had served as White House budget director.

"On an issue like earmarks, the truth of the matter is that as a budget matter, they're insignificant," Bolten told me. "If you total up all of the earmarks in the entire budget, you know, it's a percent or so of entire spending. And most earmarks are actually perfectly okay. In other words, they're not wasteful spending, they're not the bridge to nowhere. And so as a budget matter, you're not making a major policy mistake by winking at them. As a political matter, you may be. And you dispirit a lot of people who care most about the party's roots. And you give them the misimpression that because you winked at the bridge to nowhere, you don't care about spending. So it may be that in the end, historians may say that was an error. If it was, I think it was more of a political error than a substantive error. Because the record of political conservatism through those years is pretty strong. And the president took some pretty tough positions on non–security related spending."

Bolten said skittish Republicans, especially in the House, believed they could save their seats by bringing home pork-barrel spending to their districts. But in the process, they may have hurt their party nationally. "Because the margins were so narrow, and because the Hill leadership correctly perceived that our majority was in jeopardy, that may almost have triggered the wrong kind of reaction," he said. "Which is, 'We have to do what we need to do to make sure that individual members are able to campaign on something that's happy for them back home,' rather than 'We need to look good as a party properly moored to its roots.' So the leadership was more interested in making sure that a member had a project or an earmark or something like that to take back home, which I think individually may be wise, but collectively may have constituted a major error. As the White House, we were not supportive of that approach. I mean, as budget director, I wouldn't support it. I'd have gladly gotten rid of lots of projects and earmarks and things like that. On the other hand, we were supportive of the leadership. And I think we correctly valued our relationship with the leadership more highly than we did purity on any individual earmark."

Republican National Committee chairman Ken Mehlman said excessive spending and a flurry of scandals combined to dissolve the glue that had held the GOP's narrow majority together for years. "Without reform, conservatism is a minority philosophy," he told me. "With reform, it can become a majority philosophy. Think about it: what separates Reagan and Goldwater is that Reagan is seen as a reformer and is therefore able to win lots of swing voters," he said. "The reason that the Contract With America was such an important document was that it combined conservatism and reform."

And now, a dozen years later, the abandonment of reform had contributed to a Republican loss of thirty seats in the House and half a dozen in the Senate. Karl Rove tried to console himself with the knowledge that such losses were typical for any political party that had held the White House for six years. Cheney, on the other hand, was heartened to see prowar senator Joe Lieberman beat antiwar challenger Ned Lamont, even after Lieberman had been abandoned by the Democratic Party. "He won anyway—as an independent, which was nice," the vice president told me. "So I think that makes Joe pretty independent these days. I mean, he's an honest to goodness independent."

Shortly after the election, Cheney encountered his former vice presidential rival at a White House meeting. Cheney leaned over to Lieberman at the cabinet table and remarked that being one of only two independents in a closely divided Senate must "be better than being vice president." Lieberman smiled and replied that Cheney was just trying to make him feel good about his loss in 2000.

Bush also tried to maintain a sense of humor about losing control of Congress for the first time in his presidency. In fact, he began his post-election press conference in the East Room with an inside joke. "Why all the glum faces?" he asked the White House reporters, knowing they were actually pleased with the outcome. "The election is over and the Democrats won," he acknowledged. "It was a thumpin'."

Bush said he had believed, right up to the end, despite warning signs from public opinion polls, that Republicans would retain control of Congress. "I knew we were going to lose seats, I just didn't know how many," he explained. "I thought when it was all said and done, the American people would understand the importance of taxes and the importance of security."

Noting that off-year elections were often decided by the economy, the president had clung to the hope that voters would reward Republicans for keeping taxes low and the economy strong. But the press had given Bush almost no credit for his successful economic policies, preferring to focus almost exclusively on his troubled Iraq policy.

"The good news in the economy was overwhelmed by the toughness of this fight and toughness of the war," Bush said. "Surprised me somewhat—which goes to show I should not try punditry."

Bush had already placed a congratulatory call to House Minority Leader Nancy Pelosi of California, who was about to become America's first female Speaker of the House. "In my first act of bipartisan outreach since the election, I shared with her the names of some Republican interior decorators who can help her pick out the new drapes in her new offices," the president joked.

A CNN reporter reminded Bush that "Pelosi has called you 'incompetent,' a 'liar,' the 'emperor with no clothes,' and as recently as yesterday, 'dangerous.'" But the president was in a forgiving mood.

"I've been around politics a long time; I understand when campaigns end, and I know when governing begins," he said. "Look, people say unfortunate things at times. But if you hold grudges in this line of work, you're never going to get anything done."

Indeed, Bush did not hold a grudge against George Allen or the other Republicans who had squandered the party's majority. "Our reputation is so much to the contrary that people find it hard to believe, but this is not an angry White House," Bolten told me. "And it comes from the president. He is not an angry guy. He's an aggressive guy, but whatever is past is past. He doesn't look back, he doesn't point fingers. And we say that stuff and people think, 'Oh yeah, you got your talking points and you drink the Kool-Aid.' It's actually true. He may think somebody's just a total idiot who screwed up unbelievably badly, but he's not really focused on it and he's not even really going to take it out on that person."

Instead, Bush took some of the blame himself, even though he had not been on the ballot. "I'm obviously disappointed with the outcome of the election, and as the head of the Republican Party, I share a large part of the responsibility," he said. "No question Iraq had something to do with it. And it's tough, in a time of war, when people see carnage on their television screens."

He acknowledged he had failed to adequately articulate his willingness to adjust tactics in response to the evolving threat in Iraq. Consequently, many Americans voted "to register their displeasure with the lack of progress being made" in Iraq, he said. "Somehow it seeped in their conscious that my attitude was just simply 'stay the course,'" he said. "'Stay the course' means let's get the job done. But it doesn't mean staying stuck on a strategy or tactics that may not be working. So perhaps I need to do a better job of explaining that we're constantly adjusting."

While Bush had struggled to articulate his Iraq policy, Democrats had skillfully eroded public support for the war. Polls showed the percentage of voters who approved of the decision to go to war in Iraq had slipped from a majority in 2004 to a minority in 2006.

"I do understand the heart of the people," the president said. "I understand they're frustrated. I am too. I wish this had gone faster. So does Secretary Rumsfeld," he added. "Now, after a series of thoughtful conversations, Secretary Rumsfeld and I agreed that the timing is right for new leadership at the Pentagon."

Reporters rightfully questioned Bush about why, just days earlier, he had assured them Rumsfeld would be staying on through the end of the president's term.

"I didn't want to inject a major decision about this war in the final days of a campaign. And so the only way to answer that question and to get you on to another question was to give you that answer," Bush explained. "It sends a bad signal to our troops if they think the commander in chief is constantly adjusting tactics and decisions based upon politics. And I think it's important in a time of war that, to the extent possible, we leave politics out of the major decisions being made."

The other reason for the president's lack of candor was that he had not yet met with Rumsfeld's designated replacement, former CIA director Bob Gates. Nor had Bush and Rumsfeld finalized their decision on the shakeup, reached during a conversation on election day, before any results were known.

The media's pique over being misled was dwarfed by its satisfaction over Rumsfeld's ouster. So the real outrage over Bush's post-election bombshell came from not reporters, but congressional Republicans. The anger was so widespread that it forced Bolten to abandon his plans to travel with the president to Vietnam. "I stayed behind to basically take incoming from Republicans. I had four or five lunches down in the mess and the Ward Room and basically just let people ventilate," Bolten told me. "I think some members were looking for something or somebody to blame and this sort of crystallized it. You know, 'The White House just didn't get it about how unpopular the war and Rumsfeld were. And then they let him go the day after the election. How could they do that?'"

Bolten added, "The first thing out of anyone's mouth is, 'What were you thinking? Why did you let Rumsfeld go the day after the election? If you had done this a month before the election, it would have helped me enormously.' It would have looked like the cheesiest political maneuver on the planet and would have undermined something that the president cherishes, which is the confidence of the military, up and down the line. He cherishes that, and it's something that I forget about often, but he always reminds us as he's working on a speech draft. He says, 'I'm talking to not just the American people here, but I'm talking to Iraqis, I'm talking to our enemies, and most importantly, I'm talking to our troops when I give a speech. If anybody's listening to what I say about the war in Iraq, it's got to be them.'"

Sure enough, at his post-election press conference, Bush explicitly warned each of these audiences not to read too much into the Democratic takeover of Congress. "To our brave men and women in uniform: Don't be doubtful. America will always support you. Our nation is blessed to have men and women who volunteer to serve, and are willing to risk their own lives for the safety of our fellow citizens," he vowed. "To the people of Iraq: Do not be fearful. As you take the difficult steps toward democracy and peace, America is going to stand with you. We know you want a better way of life, and now is the time to seize it."

Bush had ominous words for the terrorists. "To our enemies: Do not be joyful. Do not confuse the workings of our democracy with a lack of will. Our nation is committed to bringing you to justice. Liberty and democracy are the source of America's strength, and liberty and democracy will lift up the hopes and desires of those you are trying to destroy."

Bush was not the only leader to publicly address his various audiences in this manner. So did Osama bin Laden's second in command, Ayman al-Zawahiri, who issued a post-election "message to the Democrats in America."

"You aren't the ones who won the midterm elections," said the al Qaeda leader in an audiotape. "Nor are the Republicans the ones who lost. Rather, the *mujahideen*—the Muslim people's vanguard in Afghanistan and Iraq—are the ones who won, and the American forces and their crusader allies are the ones who lost." He added, "The mujahideen won't stop inflicting losses on you until you leave our lands, stop plundering our treasures, and stop backing the corrupt rulers in our countries."

Not wanting the GOP to feel left out, al-Zawahiri then broadened his message to encompass a bipartisan audience. "I tell both the Republicans and Democrats: you are attempting in panic to find a way out of the disasters which surround you in Iraq and Afghanistan," he said. He mocked America's anguished debate over when and how to withdraw troops from these conflicts. He predicted the U.S. would eventually negotiate pullout agreements with the fledgling democratic governments in Baghdad and Kabul, only to be forced to return by the resulting chaos in both nations. It was eerily reminiscent of Bush's own argument that if the U.S. withdrew too soon, it would be compelled to return in much graver circumstances. "You shall come back," he warned, "with no other choice but to negotiate with the real powers."

Broadening his audience even further, the terrorist then delivered "a message to the American people." "I say to them: you only realized the failure of the administration and toppled the Republicans' candidates after the mujahideen slaughtered you," he bragged. "And I tell them: Bush reflects the level of thought of the American nation, despite all the research centers, specialists, thinkers, and historians it has. A nation which chooses Bush as its president is a nation of negligible morals, ideology, and intellect."

Setting aside such ad hominem attacks, Bush agreed with al-Zawahiri about the long-term dangers to America. "If we were to leave before the job is done, the country becomes more at risk," he told the reporters in the East Room. "If the job is not complete, al Qaeda will have safe haven from which to launch attacks. These radicals and extremists have made it clear they want to topple moderate governments to spread their ideology. They believe that it's just a matter of time before we leave so they can implement their strategies. We're just not going to let them do that. We're going to help this government become a government that can defend, govern, and sustain itself, and an ally in the war on terror."

In other words, Bush was determined to press ahead with his policy in Iraq, despite his party's loss in Congress. "The election has changed many things in Washington, but it has not changed my fundamental responsibility, and that is to protect the American people from attack. As the commander in chief, I take these responsibilities seriously," he said. "I understand people didn't agree with some of my decisions. I'm going to continue making decisions based upon what I think is right for the country. I've never been one to try to fashion the principles I believe or the decisions I make based upon some kind of short-term popularity."

He concluded by reminding all audiences of his overarching presidential philosophy. "I didn't come to Washington just to occupy the office," he said. "I came to get some positive things done on behalf of the country."

Chapter Ten

"THE AUTHOR OF LIBERTY"

FOR A SECULAR DICTATOR, Saddam Hussein sure made a point of saying his prayers as he was led to the gallows.

"God is great," he murmured as he was positioned over the trap door by guards wearing black ski masks.

Saddam did not want a hood placed over his head, so the guards wrapped it around his neck in advance of the noose. Thrilled by the imminent death of Iraq's top Sunni, some of the Shiite guards began chanting the name of radical Shiite cleric Moqtada al-Sadr.

"Moqtada! Moqtada! Moqtada!"

"Moqtada?" Saddam asked contemptuously. "Is this how real men behave? Is this the bravery of Arabs?"

One of the Shiite guards replied by invoking the name of al-Sadr's father-in-law, who was tortured and killed by Saddam's regime in 1980.

"Long live Muhammad Baqir al-Sadr!"

The taunts and ripostes continued as the bulky noose with seven coils was draped around Saddam's neck.

"Go to hell," a guard advised the former dictator.

"The hell that is Iraq?" Saddam queried.

"God damn you!" said a guard.

"God damn *you*!" retorted Saddam, calling the platform on which he stood a "gallows of shame."

"You have destroyed us, killed all of us," a guard lamented. "Our nation is ruined!"

"I helped you survive," Saddam countered as a guard cinched the noose snug around his neck. "Iraq is nothing without me!"

This exchange was too much for one guard, who beseeched his colleagues to stop engaging the doomed dictator. "Please do not. The man is being executed," the guard implored. "Please no, I beg you to stop."

Mindful that his last moments of life were slipping away, Saddam began to murmur the Islamic creed, or *shahadah*, as he stood on the platform, his hands bound behind his back. "There is no God but Allah and I testify that Muhammad is the messenger of God," he said. "There is no God but Allah and I testify that Muhammad—"

Suddenly the trap door crashed open, and the sixty-nine-year-old despot dropped like a stone through the gallows. The rope went taut, and Saddam's neck snapped audibly.

"The tyrant has fallen!" a guard exclaimed amid a cacophony of excited voices. "May God curse him!"

The once omnipotent ruler of Iraq now dangled ignominiously from the end of a rope. The ex-dictator with the blood of a million Muslims on his hands stared through lifeless eyes at the concrete ceiling of his primitive death chamber. It was a momentous turning point for Iraq. On December 30, 2006, three years after he had been dragged from a spider hole by American troops, Saddam Hussein was dead.

Found guilty of massacring 148 men and boys at Dujail nearly a quarter century earlier, Saddam was never tried for his other crimes against humanity. Once he was sentenced to death, there was no point in going to the trouble of additional trials. After the initial verdict was upheld by an appeals court, the execution was carried out with a swiftness that startled most Americans, who were accustomed to decades of appeals by death row inmates. Iraqis took to the streets to celebrate the death of arguably the most evil man on the planet.

Naturally, the American press was horrified. Most journalists opposed the death penalty, even for a monster like Saddam, so they played up the chaotic and undignified nature of his hanging. (The outrage intensified when an overly long hangman's rope severed the head of Saddam's half-brother, Barzan al-Tikriti, the sadist in red cowboy boots who had laid siege to Dujail.) Even Bush was irked by the indiscretion of Saddam's executioners, although he considered this a minor blemish on an otherwise historic accomplishment.

"Today, Saddam Hussein was executed after receiving a fair trial—the kind of justice he denied the victims of his brutal regime," the president said.

Still, Bush was unable to muster much enthusiasm. Saddam's death came on the same day that the number of American soldiers killed in Iraq reached three thousand. All the optimism of a year earlier, when twelve million Iraqi voters had braved terrorist threats to choose the nation's first democratically elected government, now seemed a cruel joke. Vice President Cheney had hailed 2005 as the "watershed year," the "turning point" in Iraq's struggle to quash the insurgency. When he made those remarks to ABC's Terry Moran during a visit to al-Anbar province in December 2005, most observers were predicting that the U.S. would be able to begin reducing troop levels in Iraq by the end of 2006. Indeed, on that same December day, Bush himself gave a prime-time address to the nation in which he expressed hope that within a year's time, the mission in Iraq "should require fewer American troops." Well, a year had now passed and the only talk of troop reductions came from those who had given up on the war, not those who believed the security situation allowed for a drawdown. Instead of subsiding, the violence in Iraq had intensified throughout 2006, thanks to the February bombing of the Golden Mosque in Samarra. As for "Operation Together Forward," the Baghdad security plan Bush had announced upon his triumphant return from Baghdad seven months earlier, it had utterly failed to quell the burgeoning violence.

Bush was now painfully aware that the U.S. effort in Iraq was fundamentally flawed. He commissioned studies by the Joint Chiefs of Staff and the National Security Council to find a better way forward. He scrutinized the recommendations of a bipartisan entity known as the Iraq Study Group, which concluded in December 2006 that "the situation in Iraq is grave and deteriorating." He met with members of Congress from both parties at the White House to solicit their recommendations. After much consultation and soul searching, the president announced a major change in course during a televised address to the nation on January 10, 2007. He began by eating a major helping of crow—in prime time.

"When I addressed you just over a year ago, nearly twelve million Iraqis had cast their ballots for a unified and democratic nation," he said from the White House Library. "The elections of 2005 were a stunning achievement. We thought that these elections would bring the Iraqis together, and that as we trained Iraqi security forces we could accomplish our mission with fewer American troops. But in 2006 the opposite happened. The violence in Iraq—particularly in Baghdad—overwhelmed the political gains the Iraqis had made. Al Qaeda terrorists and Sunni insurgents recognized the mortal danger that Iraq's elections posed for their cause, and they responded with outrageous acts of murder aimed at innocent Iraqis. They blew up one of the holiest shrines in Shia Islam—the Golden Mosque of Samarra—in a calculated effort to provoke Iraq's Shiite population to retaliate. Their strategy worked. Radical Shia elements, some supported by Iran, formed death squads. And the result was a vicious cycle of sectarian violence that continues today. The situation in Iraq is unacceptable to the American people—and it is unacceptable to me. Our troops in Iraq have fought bravely. They have done everything we have asked them to do. Where mistakes have been made, the responsibility rests with me. It is clear that we need to change our strategy in Iraq."

Bush was remarkably candid about the old strategy's shortcomings, especially the lack of sufficient troops in Baghdad. "Iraqi and American forces cleared many neighborhoods of terrorists and insurgents, but when our forces moved on to other targets, the killers returned," he explained. "This time, we'll have the force levels we need to hold the areas that have been cleared."

To that end, Bush announced he would "surge" at least 20,000 additional troops into Iraq. Around 4,000 would be sent to the deadly Anbar province, while the remainder would go to Baghdad, as 80 percent of Iraq's sectarian violence occurred within thirty miles of the capital. The American troop contingent in Iraq already numbered 138,000—the level had fluctuated between 115,00 and 160,000 over the previous three and a half years. Thus, it could be argued the president's "surge" was merely a routine fluctuation, made in response to conditions on the ground. But Bush was under intense pressure to demonstrate he was making a fundamental change in his Iraq policy. And, to be fair, his new policy went beyond a simple surge of troops. He also promised to lift restrictions undermining soldiers who would crack down on well-connected Shiite militants.

"In earlier operations, political and sectarian interference prevented Iraqi and American forces from going into neighborhoods that are home to those fueling the sectarian violence," the president acknowledged. "This time, Iraqi and American forces will have a green light to enter those neighborhoods. And Prime Minister Maliki has pledged that political or sectarian interference will not be tolerated."

Bush also promised to hold the Iraqis accountable to "benchmarks" of reform. He predicted Baghdad would pass laws to distribute oil revenues among all Iraqis and ease a ban on former members of Saddam's Baath Party. U.S. forces would also accelerate training of Iraqi army and police units. Bush promised a crackdown on Iran and Syria, both of which were providing weapons and training to Iraqi insurgents. These rogue regimes allowed terrorists to freely move back and forth across their borders with Iraq.

"We'll interrupt the flow of support from Iran and Syria. And we will seek out and destroy the networks providing advanced weaponry and training to our enemies in Iraq," Bush vowed. "I recently ordered the deployment of an additional carrier strike group to the region. We will expand intelligence-sharing and deploy Patriot air defense systems to reassure our friends and allies."

Mindful that newly empowered Democrats were growing bolder in their demands for withdrawing U.S. troops, Bush warned that "failure in Iraq would be a disaster for the United States." To drive home his point, he spelled out the consequences of such a failure.

"To step back now would force a collapse of the Iraqi government, tear the country apart, and result in mass killings on an unimaginable scale. Such a scenario would result in our troops being forced to stay in Iraq even longer, and confront an enemy that is even more lethal," he predicted. "The consequences of failure are clear: radical Islamic extremists would grow in strength and gain new recruits. They would be in a better position to topple moderate governments, create chaos in the region, and use oil revenues to fund their ambitions. Iran would be emboldened in its pursuit of nuclear weapons. Our enemies would have a safe haven from which to plan and launch attacks on the American people. On September the eleventh, 2001, we saw what a refuge for extremists on the other side of the world could bring to the streets of our own cities. For the safety of our people, America must succeed in Iraq," he exhorted. "If we increase our support at this crucial moment, and help the Iraqis break the current cycle of violence, we can hasten the day our troops begin coming home."

Bush was not about to repeat the mistake of a year earlier, when he expressed hope that by the end of 2006, the Iraq mission "should require fewer American troops." This time around, he played it much safer by merely voicing a desire to "hasten the day our troops begin coming home."

Nor was the president willing to make any hard-and-fast predictions about the surge reducing violence—at least not right away. "Let me be clear: the terrorists and insurgents in Iraq are without conscience, and they will make the year ahead bloody and violent. Even if our new strategy works exactly as planned, deadly acts of violence will continue—and we must expect more Iraqi and American casualties," he cautioned. "This new strategy will not yield an immediate end to suicide bombings, assassinations, or IED [improvised explosive device] attacks. Our enemies in Iraq will make every effort to ensure that our television screens are filled with images of death and suffering. Yet over time, we can expect to see Iraqi troops chasing down murderers, fewer brazen acts of terror, and growing trust and cooperation from Baghdad's residents," he ventured. "When this happens, daily life will improve, Iraqis will gain confidence in their leaders, and the government will have the breathing space it needs to make progress in other critical areas. Most of Iraq's Sunni and Shia want to live together in peace—and reducing the violence in Baghdad will help make reconciliation possible."

Having sketched out the implications for Iraq, Bush now broadened his argument to encompass the entire region. "The challenge playing out across the broader Middle East is more than a military conflict. It is the decisive ideological struggle of our time. On one side are those who believe in freedom and moderation. On the other side are extremists who kill the innocent, and have declared their intention to destroy our way of life. In the long run, the most realistic way to protect the American people is to provide a hopeful alternative to the hateful ideology of the enemy, by advancing liberty across a troubled region. It is in the interests of the United States to stand with the brave men and women who are risking their lives to claim their freedom, and to help them as they work to raise up just and hopeful societies across the Middle East."

Bush made clear that those societies would be affected by the success or failure of America's mission in Iraq. "From Afghanistan to Lebanon to the Palestinian territories, millions of ordinary people are sick of the violence and want a future of peace and opportunity for their children. And they are looking at Iraq. They want to know: Will America withdraw and yield the future of that country to the extremists? Or will we stand with the Iraqis who have made the choice for freedom?"

Bush, who regularly met with the families of fallen soldiers, could not conclude this speech to tens of millions of Americans without paying tribute to the military. "In these dangerous times, the United States is blessed to have extraordinary and selfless men and women willing to step forward and defend us. These young Americans understand that our cause in Iraq is noble and necessary—and that the advance of freedom is the calling of our time. They serve far from their families, who make the quiet sacrifices of lonely holidays and empty chairs at the dinner table. They have watched their comrades give their lives to ensure our liberty. We mourn the loss of every fallen American—and we owe it to them to build a future worthy of their sacrifice."

Hoping to appeal to the public's higher ideals, the president closed by invoking the sweep of history. "Fellow citizens, the year ahead will demand more patience, sacrifice, and resolve. It can be tempting to think that America can put aside the burdens of freedom. Yet times of testing reveal the character of a nation. And throughout our history, Americans have always defied the pessimists and seen our faith in freedom redeemed. Now America is engaged in a new struggle that will set the course for a new century. We can, and we will, prevail. We go forward with trust that the Author of Liberty will guide us through these trying hours."

Chapter Eleven

"The Creator of Life"

Fifteen months after President Bush replaced moderate Sandra Day O'Connor with conservative Samuel Alito on the Supreme Court, the move began to pay major dividends. On April 18, 2007, the Court issued its most significant abortion ruling since *Roe v. Wade*, the landmark 1973 case that effectively established abortion as a constitutional right. With Alito casting the crucial vote, the Court ruled 5–4 to uphold the federal partial-birth abortion ban, which Bush had signed into law back in 2003. It was the first time the high court allowed a ban on a specific type of abortion. The seismic ruling was simultaneously cheered by pro-lifers and denounced by pro-choicers as a major shift by the Court, which was now headed by Chief Justice John Roberts, another Bush appointee. Indeed, a third of a century after the abortion pendulum had swung dramatically to the left, the young Roberts Court was now clearly pushing it defiantly back to the right. In doing so, the Court aligned itself with the overwhelming majority of Americans who abhorred the gruesome practice of partial-birth abortion.

That gruesomeness was graphically conveyed by Justice Anthony Kennedy, the Court's lone moderate, in the decision he wrote for the majority, which included the four conservatives, Roberts, Alito, Antonin Scalia, and Clarence Thomas. In order to place partial-birth abortion in the proper context, Kennedy began by describing another late-term abortion procedure not banned by the act.

"The doctor, often guided by ultrasound, inserts grasping forceps through the woman's cervix and into the uterus to grab the fetus," Kennedy wrote. "The doctor grips a fetal part with the forceps and pulls it back through the cervix and vagina, continuing to pull even after meeting resistance from the cervix. The friction causes the fetus to tear apart. For example, a leg might be ripped off the fetus as it is pulled through the cervix and out of the woman. The process of evacuating the fetus piece by piece continues until it has been completely removed."

Kennedy then explained that partial-birth abortion was different. "The doctor extracts the fetus in a way conducive to pulling out its entire body, instead of ripping it apart," he wrote.

But Kennedy's description could not begin to capture the monstrous reality of partial-birth abortion, and so he cited an infamous medical paper written in 1992 by Dr. Martin Haskell, who had performed the ghastly procedure hundreds of times.

"Most surgeons find dismemberment at twenty weeks and beyond to be difficult due to the toughness of fetal tissues at this stage of development," Haskell explained.

In other words, the baby's bones and sinews have grown so strong by the second half of a pregnancy that doctors have trouble ripping them apart in the womb. It's less work to simply pull the baby's body out intact. That, according to Haskell, was the beauty of partial-birth abortion.

"It does not rely upon dismemberment to remove the fetus," he wrote. "Rather, the surgeon grasps and removes a nearly intact fetus."

To that end, the abortionist uses ultrasound to locate the baby's legs—or "lower extremities," to use the clinical euphemism employed by Haskell, who likewise referred to arms as "upper extremities."

"The surgeon introduces a large grasping forcep," he wrote. "He moves the tip of the instrument carefully towards the fetal lower extremities. When the instrument appears on the sonogram screen, the surgeon is able to open and close its jaws to firmly and reliably grasp a lower extremity."

This allows the abortionist to yank a leg out through the mother's vagina without actually tearing it from the rest of the baby.

"With a lower extremity in the vagina, the surgeon uses his fingers to deliver the opposite lower extremity, then the torso, the shoulders and the upper extremities," Haskell wrote.

At this point, the baby's head gets stuck because the mother's cervix is not sufficiently dilated. This is fortunate for the abortionist because if the head somehow managed to pop out of the cervix the baby would be born. And once the baby is born, killing it would be illegal. But as long as the head stays lodged in the cervix—even though the rest of the body is outside the mother, wriggling with life—the abortionist could legally kill it (that is, until the Supreme Court upheld the Partial-Birth Abortion Ban Act). Haskell chillingly described the final step in killing the baby as it struggled, face down, for life.

"At this point, the right-handed surgeon slides the fingers of the left hand along the back of the fetus and 'hooks' the shoulders of the fetus with the index and ring fingers (palm down). Next he slides the tip of the middle finger along the spine towards the skull," he wrote. "The surgeon takes a pair of blunt curved Metzenbaum scissors in the right hand. He carefully advances the tip, curved down, along the spine and under his middle finger until he feels it contact the base of the skull under the tip of his middle finger. The surgeon then forces the scissors into the base of the skull," he continued. "Having safely entered the skull, he spreads the scissors to enlarge the opening. The surgeon removes the scissors and introduces a suction catheter into this hole and evacuates the skull contents."

That's a polite way of saying the abortionist sucks the baby's brains out. Once the child is dead, the doctor can pull its head out of the cervix and throw away a brainless but otherwise intact human being without fear of being charged with murder.

Having related "an abortion doctor's clinical description," Kennedy then cited a less clinical account by a nurse who had witnessed Haskell abort a baby who was partially born to his mother halfway through her twenty-seventh week of pregnancy.

"Dr. Haskell went in with forceps and grabbed the baby's legs and pulled them down into the birth canal. Then he delivered the baby's body and the arms—everything but the head. The doctor kept the head right inside the uterus," the nurse testified before the Senate Judiciary Committee. "The baby's little fingers were clasping and unclasping, and his little feet were kicking. Then the doctor stuck the scissors in the back of his head, and the baby's arms jerked out, like a startle reaction, like a flinch, like a baby does when he thinks he is going to fall. The doctor opened up the scissors, stuck a high-powered suction tube into the opening, and sucked the baby's brains out. Now the baby went completely limp," she concluded. "He cut the umbilical cord and delivered the placenta. He threw the baby in a pan, along with the placenta and the instruments he had just used."

Thanks to Bush, such an atrocity would now land a doctor in prison for up to two years. Although only a small percentage of the 1.3 million abortions performed each year were of the partial-birth variety, the number was certainly in the thousands. Perhaps in most of those cases, doctors would still kill the babies by tearing them apart in the womb or resorting to other grisly techniques sidestepping the ban on partial-birth abortion. And yet it was not unreasonable to assume that, over time, the ban would save at least a few lives. Those human beings, in a very real sense, would owe their lives to George W. Bush, the evangelical president who believed each life was sacred. It was Bush, after all, who had signed the ban on partial-birth abortion in the first place and then installed Supreme Court justices who would uphold that ban. Of course, Bush was politically astute enough to downplay the religious ramifications of his actions.

"When I interviewed the Supreme Court justices I didn't quiz them on their religion or their morality," he told me. "I quizzed them on their view of the Constitution."

Bush's predecessor, Bill Clinton, twice vetoed partial-birth abortion bans in the 1990s. Although most polls showed that two-thirds of Americans favored a ban, Clinton said he rejected the legislation because it made no exception for the health of the mother. Pro-lifers considered this argument disingenuous, because the bans did contain an exception for the life of the mother. And if the mother's life wasn't threatened by the pregnancy, what other health consideration could possibly justify a procedure as barbaric as partial-birth abortion? Also, the definition of the health of the mother was determined in another abortion case, *Doe v. Bolton*, as including emotional, psychological, familial, and age factors. Truth be told, liberals insisted on a "health of the mother" exception because it amounted to a much lower threshold than "life of the mother" and thus gave abortionists enormous leeway for abuse. In every run-of-the-mill late-term pregnancy, a doctor would be able to legally justify partial-birth abortion merely by asserting that dismemberment in the womb posed at least a minor risk to the mother's health. Mindful of this sham, the Republican Congress intentionally kept the "health of the mother" exception out of the 2003 version of the ban. This omission, which had been veto bait to Clinton, was a blessing to Bush. He signed the bill with relish.

"For years, a terrible form of violence has been directed against children who are inches from birth, while the law looked the other way," the president told a pro-life audience at a signing ceremony in the Ronald Reagan Building in Washington. "Today, at last, the American people and our government have confronted the violence and come to the defense of the innocent child."

The crowd erupted in cheers and applause. When Bush tried to thank the audience for working so hard to build support for the ban, someone shouted out, "Thank *you*, Mr. President!" The place erupted again.

"The best case against partial-birth abortion is a simple description of what happens and to whom it happens. It involves the partial delivery of a live boy or girl, and a sudden, violent end of that life. Our nation owes its children a different and better welcome," Bush said. "America stands for liberty, for the pursuit of happiness, and for the unalienable right of life. And the most basic duty of government is to defend the life of the innocent. Every person, however frail or vulnerable, has a place and a purpose in this world. Every person has a special dignity. This right to life cannot be granted or denied by government, because it does not come from government. It comes from the Creator of life."

It was Bush at his most evangelical. Convinced that God bestowed fundamental rights upon all people, the president saw abortion as the ultimate abrogation of those rights. In wielding his presidential power to begin limiting abortion, he was demonstrating the very essence of evangelism—the notion that Christian faith should inform and shape public policy on the most profound moral questions vexing the nation. Besides, as far as Bush was concerned, upholding the ideals of Christianity and being a good American happened to be one and the same.

"In the debate about the rights of the unborn, we are asked to broaden the circle of our moral concern. We're asked to live out our calling as Americans. We're asked to honor our own standards, announced on the day of our founding in the Declaration of Independence. We're asked by our convictions and tradition and compassion to build a culture of life and make this a more just and welcoming society. And today, we welcome vulnerable children into the care and protection of Americans," the president said. "By acting to prevent this practice, the elected branches of our government have affirmed a basic standard of humanity, the duty of the strong to protect the weak. The wide agreement amongst men and women on this issue, regardless of political party, shows that bitterness in political debate can be overcome by compassion and the power of conscience."

The president's lofty rhetoric back in 2003 was tempered by the cold realization that the ban would almost certainly be struck down by federal judges. After all, a federal judge in 1998 had declared a similar ban in Nebraska to be unconstitutional. That ruling was eventually appealed to the Supreme Court, which upheld the lower court in 2000, striking down the ban with a 5–4 decision, the crucial vote being cast by Justice O'Connor. Three years later, when Bush signed the nationwide ban, of course he had no way of knowing that by the time the law reached the Supreme Court, he would have replaced O'Connor with Alito, who once wrote that "the Constitution does not protect a right to an abortion." All Bush knew back in 2003 was that he would do everything in his power to make the ban the law of the land, despite the expected court challenges. So he urged pro-lifers not to be discouraged by the difficult legal path ahead. He assured them they would win in the end.

"The facts about partial-birth abortion are troubling and tragic, and no lawyer's brief can make them seem otherwise," he said. "The executive branch will vigorously defend this law against any who would try to overturn it in the courts."

Sure enough, the ban was immediately declared unconstitutional by federal judges in New York, California, and Nebraska, all of whom objected to the lack of an exception for a woman's health. The Bush administration spent the next three years appealing the case all the way to Supreme Court, which heard arguments in November 2006, ten months after Alito joined the Court. In April 2007, the Court upheld the ban with an unapologetically pro-life ruling, sending shock waves through the abortion industry.

"Respect for human life finds an ultimate expression in the bond of love the mother has for her child," Kennedy wrote. "Whether to have an abortion requires a difficult and painful moral decision. While we find no reliable data to measure the phenomenon, it seems unexceptionable to conclude some women come to regret their choice to abort the infant life they once created and sustained. Severe depression and loss of esteem can follow."

These effects were particularly devastating to women who underwent partial-birth abortion without fully understanding the heinous nature of the procedure, Kennedy noted. "It is self-evident that a mother who comes to regret her choice to abort must struggle with grief more anguished and sorrow more profound when she learns, only after the event, what she once did not know: that she allowed a doctor to pierce the skull and vacuum the fast-developing brain of her unborn child, a child assuming the human form."

This was too much for Linda Greenhouse of the *New York Times*, the most influential Supreme Court reporter in the nation. Greenhouse had never made any secret of her staunch liberalism in general and her ardent advocacy for abortion in particular. In 1989, she was reprimanded by the *Times* for actively participating in a pro-abortion march in Washington. In 2006, she used a speech at Harvard, her alma mater, to rail against the Bush administration's "sustained assault on women's reproductive freedom and the hijacking of public policy by religious fundamentalism. To say that these last years have been dispiriting is an understatement." The outburst drew no rebuke from her editors this time around because they had moved even further to the left in the interim. Indeed, her editors gave front-page treatment to Greenhouse's incredulous reaction to Kennedy's remark that "respect for human life finds an ultimate expression in the bond of love the mother has for her child."

According to Greenhouse, this proved Kennedy believed "that a pregnant woman who chooses abortion falls away from true womanhood."

Greenhouse was equally disdainful of Kennedy's suggestion that women might actually suffer adverse effects from partial-birth abortion. "That abortion is bad for fetuses is a statement of the obvious. That it is bad for women, too, is a contested premise," she sneered. "But never until Wednesday had the Court held that an abortion procedure could be prohibited because the procedure itself, not the pregnancy, threatened a woman's health—mental health, in this case, and moral health as well."

This far-fetched "notion," according to Greenhouse, was nefariously hatched at "internal strategy sessions of the anti-abortion movement in the 1990s." She lamented that "the anti-abortion movement's new focus remained largely under the radar until it emerged full-blown in Justice Kennedy's opinion."

Instead of quoting experts on both sides of the abortion issue, Greenhouse relied solely on two fellow liberals from Yale Law School, where the reporter had earned her master's degree in 1978. Professor Reva B. Siegel mocked the court's decision to "criminalize abortion to protect women" as "beyond Alice in Wonderland." Professor Jack M. Balkin fumed against the Court's "new paternalism: either a woman is crazy when she undergoes an abortion, or she will become crazy later on." So much for fair and balanced coverage by the vaunted *New York Times*.

Other liberals suggested the Court's ruling had been dictated by the Vatican. That was the clear insinuation of an anti-Catholic column by University of Chicago law professor Geoffrey R. Stone in the *Chicago Tribune*.

"All five justices in the majority," Stone noted, "are Roman Catholic. The four justices who are not all followed clear and settled precedent."

According to Stone, a self-described liberal, the five Catholic justices "abandoned" the "long-standing principle" of allowing an exception for the health of the mother. Did they do this because they were Catholic?

"The question is too obvious to ignore," Stone hinted darkly. "Judges should be careful about imposing their personal religious beliefs on the whole of society."

It was the same charge that had been leveled against Bush every time he made a policy decision that happened to coincide with his religious beliefs. Unfazed by such criticism, the president hailed the Supreme Court's ruling as both constitutionally and morally correct.

"I am pleased that the Supreme Court upheld a law that prohibits the abhorrent procedure of partial-birth abortion," Bush said. "Today's decision affirms that the Constitution does not stand in the way of the people's representatives enacting laws reflecting the compassion and humanity of America. The partial-birth abortion ban, which an overwhelming bipartisan majority in Congress passed, and I signed into law, represents a commitment to building a culture of life in America. The Supreme Court's decision is an affirmation of the progress we have made over the past six years in protecting human dignity and upholding the sanctity of life. We will continue to work for the day when every child is welcomed in life and protected in law."

That was Bush's way of saying the ban on partial birth abortion was only the beginning. Alito and Roberts were young justices who could be expected to shape abortion policy for decades. Justices Thomas and Scalia even filed a concurring opinion that *Roe* and other abortion precedents established by the Court had "no basis in the Constitution." There seemed little doubt, even among liberals, that the outlawing of partial birth abortion was merely the first step toward the ultimate goal of overturning *Roe v. Wade* altogether. Even Linda Greenhouse of the *New York Times* conceded it was "a major victory for the Bush administration."

That victory would not have been possible without the evangelical president's unwavering belief in the sanctity of human life.

Chapter Twelve

"This War Is Lost"

"Six hundred and fifty-one days, twenty-three hours."

Vice President Cheney was telling me how much time he had left in office. He was holding a digital device given to him by White House chief of staff Josh Bolten that counted down the days, hours, minutes, and seconds remaining in the Bush presidency, which would end at noon on January 20, 2009. The device was accurate, as it was now 1 PM on April 9, 2007. It also happened to be the fourth anniversary of the fall of Baghdad.

"Four years ago," Cheney told me, "this particular day was an especially satisfying one because it marked the end of the effort to take Baghdad and to take out the Iraqi government. It was the day that the statue was toppled in downtown Baghdad."

The vice president then recounted, in broad terms, the ebb and flow of the four-year effort to stabilize Iraq. The jubilation over Saddam's ouster in April 2003. The killing of his sons, Uday and Qusay, three months later. The bloody rise of Abu Musab al-Zarqawi, who bombed the UN headquarters and Jordanian embassy in Iraq later that summer. The capture of Saddam Hussein in a spider hole in December.

Cheney lamented how the violence had continued into 2004, although at least the U.S. had been able to hand over sovereignty to Iraqis. The tentative fledgling government had begun to gather strength in 2005, the year Iraqis held three spectacularly successful elections.

But just when it appeared the U.S. mission in Iraq would succeed, of course, the bombing of the Golden Mosque in Samarra had unleashed massive sectarian violence. The strife overshadowed a series of significant milestones in 2006, including the formation of a permanent unity government and the deaths of Abu Musab al-Zarqawi and Saddam Hussein.

And now, in a last-ditch effort to make 2007 better than 2006, Bush was sending tens of thousands of additional soldiers into Baghdad and al-Anbar province. Only three months had elapsed since Bush announced the surge, which would take another ten weeks to fully implement. And yet there were already hopeful signs that the strategy was bearing fruit. On April 3, 2007, Iraq's government relaxed the curfew in Baghdad, citing improved security.

"Children have come out to play again," reported correspondent Terry McCarthy on ABC's evening newscast. "Shoppers are back in markets. A few devout souls even venture past the barbed wire to pray. Baghdad is still rocked by car bombs every day. But right in the center of the city, a small area of relative calm is starting to grow, thanks to stepped-up U.S. patrols and increased Iraqi checkpoints."

The surge was also working in al-Anbar province, prompting even the *New York Times* to take notice later that month. "Anbar province, long the lawless heartland of the tenacious Sunni Arab resistance, is undergoing a surprising transformation," the *Times* reported. "Violence is ebbing in many areas, shops and schools are reopening, police forces are growing, and the insurgency appears to be in retreat."

Ironically, Cheney was less willing than the mainstream media to express optimism about the surge. But he had deep faith in the man chosen to implement the strategy, Army general David Petraeus, who had been given command of coalition forces in Iraq in early 2007. The vice president described Petraeus as the "intellectual godfather" of a counterinsurgency strategy to send U.S. troops directly into the conflict in Iraq, instead of pulling them back to remote, heavily fortified bases, which had been the practice in 2006.

"You've got to get the guys out of their operating bases and get them out into the neighborhoods, which we're doing, with positive results," Cheney told me. "It's a different way of doing business."

Cheney explained that in the pre-surge era, "the number-one priority was to transfer authority to the Iraqis as fast as possible, in terms of getting their troops running and into the fight. And the second order of priority would have been providing security. I think we've reversed that now."

The vice president was struck by how much the Democratic position on Iraq had changed in less than eighteen months. Back in the closing days of 2005, when Cheney was planning his first visit to Iraq, most congressional Democrats had considered troop withdrawal a radical and unwise idea. A proposal for the U.S. mission in Iraq to be "terminated immediately" was crushed in the House by a vote of 403–3 in November 2005. But by March 2007, the political sands in Washington had shifted dramatically. In open defiance of the president, the Democrat-controlled House voted 218–212 to withdraw U.S. forces from Iraq by August 31, 2008. Although Bush vetoed the timetable and the Republican minority sustained the veto, Democrats were clearly emboldened by their defiance of the commander in chief after deferring to him for so long.

The about-face by individual Democrats was even more striking. Back in December 2005, Senator Hillary Rodham Clinton had proclaimed, "I reject a rigid timetable that the terrorists can exploit." She reiterated that position in June 2006, telling a crowd of booing liberals at the "Take Back America" conference that it would not be "a smart strategy" to "set a date certain" for withdrawal. But by February 2007, she changed her tune and announced her own date certain. "If we in Congress don't end this war before January of 2009, as president I will," she told another crowd of booing liberals, this one at the Democratic National Committee's winter meeting.

But no Democrat flip-flopped as blatantly as Senator Harry Reid of Nevada. In November 2006, after his party won control of Congress, Reid assured America, "We're not going to do anything to limit funding or cut off funds." But just four months later, Reid as Senate majority leader endorsed a bill to cut off funds for the war within a year. Instead of calling Reid a flip-flopper, the *Washington Post* ran a news story hailing him as a "convert."

Reid, who had once glumly predicted it would take a "miracle" for Democrats to win control of the Senate in 2006, was now giddy that such a miracle had indeed materialized. He viewed the war in nakedly political terms, calculating that Democrats could amass even greater majorities by continuing to excoriate Bush over Iraq. He came right out and admitted as much during a press conference with New York senator Charles Schumer, the campaign chief for Senate Democrats.

"We're going to pick up Senate seats as a result of this war," Reid crowed to reporters on April 12. "Senator Schumer has shown me numbers that are compelling and astounding."

A week later, Reid came right out and declared, "This war is lost."

Vice President Cheney responded by railing against Reid's "defeatism." "It is cynical to declare that the war is lost because you believe it gives you political advantage," the vice president told reporters on Capitol Hill. "Leaders should make decisions based on the security interests of our country, not on the interests of their political party."

Even liberal columnist David Broder derided Reid in the *Washington Post* as an "embarrassment." Yet there was no getting around the fact that Reid and Nancy Pelosi were calling the shots on Capitol Hill. The White House now realized that losing control of the national agenda had proven more devastating than losing control of Congress. After all, even before the election, the GOP majority was so narrow the White House had had difficulty enacting legislation. After the election, the Democratic majority was even narrower, which made legislative success for them that much tougher. Moreover, Democrats had the added burden of not controlling the White House. But at least they could determine which legislation to debate.

"What's different—and I think something of a shock to the system here—is we cannot control the agenda," Bolten told me. "And so if they want to talk about subpoenas... they can do it. They can dictate what the conversation is about and when it's going to be."

The significance of this setback was not lost on Ken Mehlman, the outgoing chairman of the Republican National Committee. "Look, 80 percent of life is not how you play the game. It's what game you play," he told me. "And so if you can dictate the terms of the debate, you can usually do a pretty good job of doing well in the debate. When you have majority control, you're able to dictate the terms of what's discussed."

No longer could the White House have cooperative discussions with the leadership of the House and Senate about the legislative agenda.

"We've gone from being able to know and discuss and plan," one senior White House official told me, "to basically having to wait for whatever the latest episodic revelation that's handed down from the mountain. It requires you to be reactive, in a tactical sense. The way to sort of get above that is to be more strategic—strategically proactive," he added. "It also requires us to rely more on the Senate than we have. In the past we used the House to drive action. Now we work with our Senate colleagues to both drive action and redirect action."

"Redirect" was the aide's polite way of saying "derail." The White House began relying on the Senate, which was slower and more deliberate than the House, to paralyze Democratic legislation. Thanks to the constant threat of a filibuster, lawmakers needed three-fifths of the Senate, or sixty votes, to get anything done. Even when Republicans had been in the majority, they were five votes short of this magic number. Well, now Democrats were *nine* votes shy of sixty, which made legislative progress for them downright excruciating.

"In the Senate, it doesn't actually make that much difference whether you've got forty-nine or fifty-one, because you need sixty to do business," Bolten told me.

By contrast, the GOP's loss of the House had a larger impact on the White House.

"It makes a huge difference, particularly in the House, where legislation is scheduled by the Speaker and by the majority," Mehlman told me. "You can have a majority of one and you have a very strong ability to decide what comes on the floor of the House."

House Speaker Nancy Pelosi, an unabashed liberal, made the most of her new power.

"Speaker Pelosi has turned out to be a stronger figure than most people expected," Bolten told me, adding that she "is a tougher disciplinarian on her party than most people expected."

Another top White House aide agreed. "What's amazing," he told me, "is that they have been able to effect discipline on people. You'll have a conversation and somebody will say, in essence, 'I'm not for the first measure that we're using for withdrawal, but I've got to vote for it because the leadership has told me I've got to. It's not where I am, but I feel obligated.' Or, 'I'm uncomfortable about the budget resolution because it's got way too much in taxes and not enough in spending restraint, but I've got to vote for it.'"

Such strong-arm tactics effectively made liberals out of Democrats who had been elected in 2006 by running as moderates. In fact, Democratic leaders in both houses of Congress "moved the party more rapidly and radically to the left on the war than you might have expected," Bolten told me. The leaders were themselves pulled leftward by their party's "netroots," the militant activists who ruled the hard-left blogs proliferating across the Internet. Influential bloggers held regular conference calls with Reid and other Democratic leaders. The netroots also exerted a powerful pull on Democratic presidential candidates like Clinton and Barack Obama.

"A lot of us probably underestimated the potency of presidential politics in all of this," Bolten explained. "The need of every candidate to remain in good stead with the Democratic Party's left wing has pretty dramatically dragged not just the candidates, but the whole party to the left."

This phenomenon was accelerated by the fact that primary elections and caucuses for the 2008 presidential cycle were scheduled earlier than ever before, forcing candidates to move quickly to please the party's liberal base.

"They have to move to the view rapidly that will satisfy the left wing of their party, and I think that's bled over into the approach of the Democratic leadership," Bolten said. "It shifted more rapidly than I thought."

The development was deeply disturbing to Mehlman, who by now had left politics to practice law. "It worries me a lot that you have an almost McGovernick approach that is behind a lot of what Democrats are thinking," he told me, referring to hippie hero and 1972 Democratic presidential nominee George McGovern. "This should not be a partisan war. This is something both parties have to deal with. We cannot win the war on terror if it is partisan."

He added, "It is critically important that both parties have very strong hawk wings in them. And I've been disappointed that there has not been a larger one manifesting itself in the Democratic Party right now."

The American public, too, was disappointed in the Democratic Congress. According to Zogby, public approval of Congress dropped to an all-time low of 14 percent in July 2007, which was twenty points lower than public approval of the president. During their first six months in power, congressional Democrats passed just half a dozen major bills, preferring to devote their energies to harassing the Bush administration. To that end, the Democratic Congress launched more than 300 investigations, conducted 600 oversight hearings, and filed 350 requests for documents and interviews. The White House had to turn over 200,000 pages of documents and hire a small army of lawyers to keep up with the demand for subpoenas of Bush aides such as Karl Rove. The president allowed some cabinet agency officials, such as Attorney General Alberto Gonzales, to testify, while invoking executive privilege to block testimony from White House officials such as former White House counsel Harriet Miers. He was convinced that many of the Democratic probes were purely partisan fishing expeditions.

Back in the West Wing, Cheney stood up behind his desk and massaged his aching leg. A month earlier, a blood clot had landed him in George Washington Hospital, where he was treated for deep venous thrombosis. I asked if the condition had returned, but he waved off the question. He remained standing as he updated me on one of his favorite subjects, the restoration of executive powers to the presidency, which we had not discussed since his first trip to Iraq. In the ensuing 20 months, the administration scored significant victories in this ongoing struggle.

Chief among these was the terrorist surveillance program, which the Democratic Congress reluctantly codified. The *New York Times* gloomily reported that the new law "broadly expanded the government's authority to eavesdrop on the international telephone calls and e-mail messages of American citizens without warrants." The paper added that the law would "sharply alter the legal limits on the government's ability to monitor millions of phone calls and e-mail messages going in and out of the United States."

In another victory, Bush forced Senator Harry Reid to eat his boastful words, "We killed the PATRIOT Act!" Reid himself ended up voting to renew the legislation, which passed despite House Democrats voting against it by a margin of nearly two to one.

Bush scored an even bigger victory in the fight over the military commissions he had created to try detainees in the war against terror. Although the Supreme Court ruled these tribunals illegal, Congress stepped in and drafted sweeping legislation to reverse that ruling. The new law went even further by giving the administration broad powers in the treatment of detainees. Democrats in both the House and Senate voted overwhelmingly against it, but Bush ended up signing it into law before the midterm election. Even the *New York Times* called it a "signal victory" for the president.

"Rather than reining in the formidable presidential powers Mr. Bush and Vice President Dick Cheney have asserted since September 11, 2001, the law gives some of those powers a solid statutory foundation," the front-page article complained. "In effect it allows the president to identify enemies, imprison them indefinitely, and interrogate them—albeit with a ban on the harshest treatment—beyond the reach of the full court reviews traditionally afforded criminal defendants and ordinary prisoners. Taken as a whole, the law will give the president more power over terrorism suspects than he had before the Supreme Court decision."

Still, it stuck in Cheney's craw that so many Democrats opposed the vital programs the U.S. needed to prosecute the war on terror. "The majority of Democrats voted against those things," he told me. "I don't want to attribute evil motives. There are a number of Democrats who never believed in those measures, a number of people who never believed in the war. And they've been consistent. But there are a significant number who did support those measures originally, and who were quick to look for the exit once the political pressure started to build. And I think that part of it is unfortunate."

Cheney accused some Democrats of trying to score political points at the expense of national security. "There are some who are against it just because we're for it, who are looking for any excuse they can come up with to try to defeat George Bush and the Republicans. Substance doesn't have much to do with it," he said. "I think it's very shortsighted on their part, because if they prevail, then ultimately they're going to have to deal with the world as it is, having opposed all of those things that have made it possible for us to be successful. One of the things that's frustrating is to see the extent to which some of my friends on the Hill have forgotten how hard we had to work to protect the nation for the last five and a half years against another attack," he told me. "You've got people up there adamantly opposed to the terrorist surveillance program or the PATRIOT Act and all of those things we've done successfully. And those programs need to be maintained, they need to be strengthened. We need to continue to operate them very aggressively if we're going to protect against further attack."

Cheney reiterated his concern that many Americans had come to see the terrorist attacks of September 11 as a once-in-a-lifetime anomaly. "And I just personally believe, with every fiber of my being, that that's a crock," he said. "That's the worst possible attitude we could have as a nation. A part of that may be because I read the intelligence reports every day."

He also read the daily news coverage by mainstream media reporters whose disdain for him had only grown since the hunting accident more than a year earlier. The press routinely grumbled that Cheney was the most powerful vice president in history. When I asked Cheney if the description was true, he joked that he was merely "the flavor of the month."

"It may be because nobody can remember the earlier vice presidents," he said with a self-deprecating chuckle. "I'll let the historians worry about that."

Yet who could forget Vice President Al Gore being put in charge of "reinventing government" by President Clinton? Or Vice President Quayle being tasked to lead the Council of Competitiveness and the National Space Council by the elder President Bush? Most vice presidents were given busy work in one or two innocuous, bureaucratic outposts. Cheney, by contrast, had an unlimited portfolio. He was Bush's consigliere, an enormously influential player in all major White House decisions. Ironically, it was his lack of interest in becoming president that made him so valuable to Bush.

"When he recruited me into the job, he said he wanted me to be an important part of the administration and a major part of his team—and he's been true to his word," Cheney told me. "I've enjoyed it."

That was more than Gerald Ford had been able to say about his own vice presidency under President Nixon. Ford, who had been a mentor to Cheney, passed away in December 2006.

"He was vice president for nine months, and he told me it was the worse nine months of his life. He hated it," Cheney told me. "That hasn't been my experience."

Chapter Thirteen

PERSPICACIOUS

T HE VOICE WAS SO POWERFUL, it was physically startling. Indeed, the brawny bass baritone filled the East Room of the White House with such soulful sorrow that President Bush could be seen wiping tears from the edges of his eyes.

> *Done a-made my vow to the Lord*
> *And I never will turn back*
> *A-ha WILL go, ah SHALL go*
> *To see what the end will be . . .*

The singer was Sergeant Alvy Powell of the U.S. Army Chorus, a bear of a man who brought so much passion to the African American spiritual that listeners were practically transported back to the antebellum South. From somewhere deep in his barrel chest, Powell managed to summon that combination of hope and suffering that defined this exquisitely American genre of music.

Sometimes I'm up, sometimes I'm down
But STILL a-mah soul is a-heavenly bound
I'll pray and pray and never stop
Until I reach that a-mountaintop . . .

Between each line that Powell sang solo, the rest of the chorus mournfully chimed in: "See what the end will be." There was not a single note of musical accompaniment and yet it was the richest sound imaginable, sending chills through the world-weary politicos in attendance. Bush and the other dignitaries sat rapt as two dozen soldiers in dress blues harmonized like a heavenly host to Powell's stirring crescendo.

Done a-opened my mouth to the Lord
And I never will turn back
A-ha WILL go, ah SHALL go
To see what the end will—be-he-he-he-ee-ee . . .

When it was over, the front row of singers parted and Powell took his place among the chorus, which fell silent behind the "blue goose," as the presidential lectern was known. Bush remained seated while a man wearing a yarmulke took the stage.

"In the midst of a difficult war, President Abraham Lincoln walked the halls of this great house and found solace, strength, and inspiration from the book of Psalms," began Rabbi Michael Siegel of Anshe Emet Synagogue in Chicago. "In fact, the image of God that President Lincoln presented at the end of the Emancipation Procla-mation was based on the vision of Psalm 145."

Siegel explained the psalm in terms that were as relevant to the war on terror as they were to the war between the states. "This psalm was President Lincoln's inspiration to unify and heal a nation suffer-ing the effects of war," he said. "On this national day of prayer, may our nation be similarly inspired to hear the unifying and inspirational message of Psalm 145 and join in the sacred covenant of action."

Even Bush's detractors had to concede Bush was a man of action. At the moment, however, he sat motionless while a tall college student in a military uniform took his turn behind the blue goose.

"Almighty God, we pause to reflect on your character as we seek wisdom for such a time as this," said Eun-Jae Yu, student chaplain of the Virginia Tech Corps of Cadets, reciting Charles Swindoll's prayer composed for the occasion. "In these unsafe days, you remain all-powerful and able to protect. In these uncertain times, you remain all-knowing, leading us to right. In the unprecedented events we're facing, you remain absolutely sovereign."

Nineteen days earlier, a deranged student had massacred thirty-two classmates and professors at Virginia Tech. Bush visited the idyllic campus to help salve the wounds in the immediate aftermath of the deadliest shooting in modern U.S. history. And now this cadet chaplain was reciprocating by delivering the 2007 Prayer for the Nation.

"We ask that you guard and guide our president and all who serve the people of these United States," Yu said. "May uncompromising integrity mark their lives.... May genuine humility return to our ranks. And may that blend of integrity and humility heal our land."

When the president finally took the stage, he cited a quotation by George Washington that left no doubt about his own view of church and state. "'It's the duty of all nations to acknowledge the providence of Almighty God, to obey His will, to be grateful for His benefits, and to humbly implore His protection and favor,'" Bush said. "It's interesting that the first president said those words. For two centuries, Americans have answered this call to prayer. We're a prayerful nation; I believe that makes us a strong nation," he asserted. "Through prayer, each of us is reminded that we are fallen creatures in need of mercy. And in seeking the mercy and compassion of a loving God, we grow in mercy and compassion ourselves."

Bush noted that prayer had many purposes, ranging from thanking God to begging forgiveness to seeking solace in the wake of tragedy. "We pray to acknowledge God's sovereignty in our lives and our complete dependence on Him," the president said. "This is probably the toughest prayer of all, particularly for those of us in politics. In the humility of prayer we recognize the limits of human strength and human wisdom. We seek the strength and wisdom that comes from above. We ask for the grace to align our hearts with His, echoing the words of scripture, 'Not my will, but thine be done.' We ask the Almighty to remain near to us and guide us in all we do. And when He is near, we are ready for all that may come to us."

It was precisely the sort of biblical reference that exasperated the Bill Mahers of the world. Bush was unapologetically deferring to a supreme being to "guide us in all we do." Granted, this was pretty unremarkable stuff for the vast majority of Americans with run-of-the-mill religious sensibilities. But it was anathema to secular liberals, who simply could not abide a president reciting, "Not my will, but thine be done." To Bush-haters, this was tantamount to the president admitting he was taking orders directly from God in the war against terrorism.

"The greatest gift we can offer anyone is the gift of our prayers, because our prayers have power beyond our imagining," Bush concluded. "Prayer has the power to change lives and to change the course of history. So on this National Day of Prayer, let us seek the Almighty with confidence and trust, because our Eternal Father inclines His ear to the voice of His children and answers our needs with love. May God bless America."

Bush stepped from behind the blue goose as the audience applauded. Among those clapping was the person some considered most likely to succeed him as president—Hillary Rodham Clinton. Even Rush Limbaugh, the enormously influential conservative commentator, told millions of radio listeners in May 2007, the same month as the prayer service, that there was an 80 percent chance of Clinton winning the White House. As the midterm elections had painfully demonstrated, the Iraq war was creating an increasingly difficult political environment for the GOP. Democrats were supremely confident that the momentum from 2006 would carry them to victory again in 2008. While Bush obviously wanted a Republican to succeed him in the White House, he now felt compelled to at least contemplate the possibility of a Democratic successor. His advisers sounded even more dubious about Republican prospects for retaining the presidency.

"It's going to be a very close election," Karl Rove told me. "We are at this narrow divide in politics."

Vice President Cheney agreed. "Could go either way," he told me. "Right now, we're sort of in the area where we're pretty evenly balanced on both sides." Cheney predicted the race to succeed Bush would be decided largely on the issue of Iraq. He said Republicans would have a much better chance if General Petraeus ultimately succeeded in his implementation of the surge. "A couple of possible outcomes here," he said. "One is, obviously, the Democrats ultimately prevail and implement the policy they claim they support. I think it will do enormous damage. On the other hand, I think, ultimately, the country would look at that and make a decision that the Democrats can't be trusted with the nation's security."

Just to be on the safe side, Bush resolved to take whatever steps were necessary to preclude Clinton or any other Democratic president from undoing his hard-fought gains in Iraq and the broader war on terror. The first indication of this strategy came at Bush's post-election press conference back in 2006, when he told reporters he wanted to "institutionalize, to the extent possible, steps necessary to make sure future presidents are capable of waging this war." I later asked him to elaborate.

"Look, I'd like to make as many hard decisions as I can make, and do a lot of the heavy lifting prior to whoever my successor is," Bush told me. "And then that person is going to have to come and look at the same data I've been looking at, and come to their own conclusion."

As an example, Bush cited his detainee program, which allowed him to keep enemy combatants imprisoned at Guantanamo Bay while they awaited adjudication. Bush was unmoved by endless criticism of this program (which the *New York Times* had grudgingly called "a signal victory" in his quest for executive authority), because he knew his successor would need it.

"I specifically talked about it, so that a candidate, and/or president, wouldn't have to deal with the issue," he told me. "The next person has got the opportunity to analyze the utility of the program and make his or her decision about whether or not it is necessary to protect the homeland. I suspect they'll find that it is necessary. But my only point to you is that it was important for me to lay it out there, so that the politics wouldn't enter into whether or not the program ought to survive beyond my period."

Moreover, the existence of such programs would at least slow any radical change in policy that a possible Democratic successor might want to implement.

"This enemy is not going away after my presidency," Bush warned at his press conference. "I think back to Harry Truman and Dwight Eisenhower. Harry Truman began the Cold War, and Eisenhower, obviously, from a different party, continued it. And I would hope that would be the spirit, that we're able to work together."

Bolten explained that Bush "often refers to the fact that Eisenhower campaigned vigorously against Truman's Cold War policies, and then ended up adopting them and implementing them very effectively." Bush embraced this historical template in hopes of maintaining some bipartisan continuity of U.S. policy on Iraq.

"He wants to put the Iraq war in a position where even a Democratic president would be in a position to sustain a legitimate presence there and help actually nurture Iraq along," Bolten told me. "Especially if it's a Democrat. He wants to create the conditions where a Democrat not only will have the leeway, but the obligation to see it out," he added. "And he's also been urging candidates, 'Don't get yourself too locked in where you stand right now. If you end up sitting where I sit, things could change dramatically.'"

As Bush reminded me, "It's different being a candidate and being the president."

With this in mind, White House officials did something extraordinary: they quietly reached out to the top Democratic presidential candidates and offered a piece of helpful advice: maintain some political wiggle room in your campaign rhetoric about Iraq. This had a noticeable effect; while the top contenders publicly called on Bush to immediately begin a drawdown of forces, they also were careful to stipulate that at least some troops should remain in or near Iraq for the foreseeable future.

"We may still have remaining vital national security interests that are important to America," Clinton explained to a labor forum for Democratic candidates in June 2007. "We cannot let al Qaeda have a staging ground in Iraq."

Her presidential rival John Edwards told the union members that U.S. forces must be stationed close to Iraq so they can re-enter if necessary. "As America pulls its combat troops out of Iraq, we're going to have to maintain a presence in the region, which means we probably need a rapid deployment force in Kuwait," he said. "If the Jordanians would allow us to station troops there, we may want to put troops in Jordan."

Unlike Edwards and Clinton, both of whom initially voted for the Iraq war, Democratic senator Barack Obama of Illinois was against it from the beginning. And yet even he cautioned against a hasty pullout. "The best option, I believe, is to make certain that we begin a phased redeployment, that we're as careful getting out as we were careless getting in," he told the labor forum.

Such statements provided a glimmer of hope to Bush, and signaled that the Democrats had taken his advice. "If you listen carefully, there are Democrats who say, 'Well, there needs to be some kind of presence,'" he told me. "And my argument to them is that's fine, but in order to get there, this surge needs to be completed." On the other hand, Bush worried that some Democratic candidates were taking a harder line against the war. "This is a highly charged environment," he told me. "There's a handful that say, get out—I mean, totally out." And yet even if such a candidate were to win the presidency, Bush figured he or she would come to their senses. "No matter who the president is, no matter what party, when they sit here in the Oval Office and seriously consider the effect of a vacuum being created in the Middle East, particularly one trying to be created by al Qaeda, they will then begin to understand the need to continue to support the young democracy," Bush told me. "The person sitting here will look at the intelligence about potential homeland scenarios and recognize that what happens overseas will matter to his or her ability to protect the country."

Bush tried to downplay the White House overtures to the Clinton and Obama campaigns. "If I were a candidate running for president in a complex world that we're in, I would be asking my national security team to touch base with the White House just to at least listen about plans, thoughts," he told me. "And by the way, as a candidate gets closer to nomination, or gets nominated, the CIA will be also briefing them. There is a series of outreaches, just to make sure that there is a smooth transition. But I wouldn't view this as anything other than being courteous to people who are interested."

I asked Bush why Clinton or Obama should take advice from a president they routinely criticized.

"First of all, I expect them to criticize me. That's one way you get elected in the Democratic primary, is to criticize the president. Nothing new about that," Bush told me. "I don't expect them to necessarily take advice from me. I would expect their insiders to at least get a

perspective about how we see things." He added, "We have an obligation to make sure that whoever is interested gets our point of view,
because you want somebody running for president to at least understand all perspectives, apart from the politics."

I asked a senior White House official the same question: how
could Clinton or Obama possibly take back-channel advice from a
president they spent so much time trashing?

"Well, first of all, if you're a presidential candidate," the official
said, "you're able to get by the public posturing that you may be
required to do, or that you fall into doing."

Translation: politicians can't be expected to actually honor their
campaign promises. Sure, Hillary kept promising to "end" the war.
But there was a certain amount of elasticity built into that promise,
depending on her definition of the word *end*.

"The other thing is, they are being advised by smart people," the
official said of the Democratic candidates. "We've got colleagues here
on the staff who have good communications with some of the
thinkers on that side. And there is a recognition by most of them that
there has to be a long-term presence by the United States," he added,
"if we hope to avoid America being brought back into the region in a
very precarious way, at a point where all-out resources are required."

The White House and the Democratic presidential campaigns
were discussing whether that long-term presence should be inside
Iraq, as Hillary preferred, or just outside, as Edwards suggested.

When I asked the official whether the Democrats were rejecting
such back-channel overtures, he replied, "No, I think they sort of welcome conversation." Besides, he added, Democrats understood the
negative consequences of moving too quickly to reverse Bush's Iraq
policy. The official reminded me that in the wake of Vietnam, antiwar Democrats "suffered for twenty-some-odd years because they
were identified as the party, when it came to national security, of
being weak. If I were a Democrat, I would not want to be in a place

where I was forcing us to withdraw in '08," he told me. "It's an election year and any bad consequences would immediately be on their heads. One of two things will happen if a Democrat gets elected president," he added. "They will either have to withdraw U.S. troops in order to remain true to the rhetoric—in which case, any consequences in the aftermath fall on their heads. Or they have to break their word, in which case they encourage fratricide on the left of their party. Now that's a thorny issue to work through."

Vice President Cheney was stoic about the possibility of a Democratic president fundamentally reversing the policies he and Bush had worked so hard to implement in Iraq. "It's the nature of the business, in a sense," he told me. "I mean, you get two terms. We were fortunate to get two terms. And I think we'll increasingly see a lot of emphasis on deciding who the next occupant of the Oval Office is going to be."

Bolten told me Bush's Iraq policy might be derailed even before the next president took office. Newly empowered Democrats in Congress had grudgingly agreed to fund the war through the end of September 2007, but after that, all bets were off. General Petraeus was scheduled to update Congress on the surge in September, although he warned lawmakers months before then that troops might have to stay through 2008. This was anathema to Democrats like Harry Reid, who pronounced the surge a failure in June, even before the last troops were in place. The White House gradually came to accept the reality that no matter how much progress Petraeus might report in September, it would not be good enough for the administration's detractors. Democrats were already fixing their sights on September 30 as the end-game and began counting down the days until funding would run out so they could force a major withdrawal of troops, who numbered 159,000 when the full surge was finally in place. It was a far cry from 2002, when "there was a bipartisan consensus to remove Saddam Hussein," Bush lamented.

"I'm not going to second-guess anybody's motives; it's just a very difficult political environment for members of Congress," the president told me. "They're worried about the different consequences of different decisions. And we're constantly listening."

But most Democrats were listening to the hard-left "netroots" who were hell-bent on ending the war. There were precious few Joe Liebermans with whom the White House could reason.

"In the ideal world, there would be a consensus, a bipartisan consensus about how to go forward," Bush told me. "Whether or not that's achievable, time will tell."

Recognizing the bleakness of the situation and seeking to avert a high-profile showdown, the White House signaled it might be willing to reduce the U.S. contingent, perhaps by as much as half, in 2008. But even that might not satisfy the hard-left liberals. So Bush, who had vowed as recently as August 2006 that "we're not leaving, so long as I'm the president," could no longer guarantee that pledge. Such was the cost of losing Congress to the Democrats. And that cost would only grow steeper if the White House followed suit.

One of the top candidates for the Democratic presidential nomination was Obama, who first met Bush in 2005, when the Illinois liberal and other senators were invited to the White House to hear the president discuss his second-term agenda. Bush took the opportunity to pull Obama aside and give him some friendly advice. Noting the newly minted senator's enormous popularity, Bush cautioned that it would make him a target for rivals on both sides of the aisle. Obama thanked Bush for the advice and later recounted the episode in a memoir, *The Audacity of Hope*. But in the same passage, Obama described Bush as a zealot whose demeanor was downright frightening when he discussed his second-term agenda.

"Suddenly it felt as if somebody in a back room had flipped a switch," Obama wrote. "The president's eyes became fixed; his voice took on the agitated, rapid tone of someone neither accustomed to nor welcoming interruption; his easy affability was replaced by an almost messianic certainty. As I watched my mostly Republican Senate colleagues hang on his every word, I was reminded of the dangerous isolation that power can bring, and appreciated the Founders' wisdom in designating a system to keep power in check."

When I quoted from this passage to Bush, the president seemed irritated to learn he had been trashed by the senator he had counseled.

"I thought I was actually showing some kindness," Bush told me indignantly. "And out of that he came with this belief?" The president added with a bit of a scowl, "He doesn't know me very well."

Bush figured Obama would be beaten in the Democratic primaries by Clinton, who was better known. "I do think she's a formidable candidate, because she's got a national presence and this is becoming a national primary," he told me. "And therefore the person with the national presence who has got the ability to raise enough money to sustain an effort in a multiplicity of sites has got a good chance to be nominated."

But Bush was convinced Clinton would come up short in the general election race against the Republican nominee. "I think our candidate can beat her, but it's going to be a tough race," he told me. "I will work to see to it that a Republican wins, and therefore don't accept the premise that a Democrat will win. I truly think the Republicans will hold the White House."

Bush aides held out hope that voters might be too weary of Clinton to vote for her by the time election day finally rolled around in November 2008. After all, by then Clinton would have eight years under her belt as an unusually high-profile senator, plus another eight as an unusually high-profile First Lady.

"This process is not going to serve her well," a senior White House official told me. "Think about it. She's going to be essentially saying, 'Elect me president after I've spent the last sixteen years in your face. And you didn't like me much when I was there last. Give me eight more years so I can be a presence in your life for twenty-four years. And Bill will be back in.' So no, I think this is not a helpful process for her."

A Gallup poll in April 2007 revealed that a majority of Americans already had a negative view of Clinton. The White House official predicted these high negatives would make it difficult for Clinton to win a general election against "a fresher, newer face" from the GOP with "slightly better numbers than that."

The official went on to say that Clinton, more than the other presidential candidates, would be hurt by the absurdly early start to the 2008 campaign cycle precisely because she had already spent so many years "in the limelight, in the public presence." Indeed, Clinton had announced her presidential candidacy a whopping twenty-two months in advance of election day with a prepackaged video she posted on the Internet in January 2007. Even before then, she had been unofficially campaigning for months. Truth be told, Clinton had begun to lay the groundwork for a White House bid the moment she won her Senate seat in 2000.

There were signs that Clinton had already begun to wear out her welcome on the campaign trail. For example, she was accused of faking a Southern accent during a speech at a Baptist church in Selma, Alabama, in March 2007.

"Nobody looks at her and says the things that she's saying is because she believes it," the White House official told me. "And she will do more things like that. There will be more equivalents of the accent at the Southern religious group. Sort of those charmingly enduring moments that she continually provides."

The official also ridiculed Democratic scenarios of Hillary rounding up more electoral votes than the last Democratic presidential nominee, John Kerry. "They say all she's got to do is find one midsized state more than Kerry got," he told me. "Well, that's assuming she can hold states that Kerry was able to." He argued Clinton might have difficulty holding Pennsylvania, which Kerry won in part because it was home to his wife, ketchup heiress Teresa Heinz Kerry. He pointed out that Republicans had chosen Minnesota, which Kerry had narrowly won, for their 2008 convention, which might give the GOP an edge.

The official was even more critical of Obama, who was challenging Clinton for the Democratic nomination. "I like the guy," he told me. "A very likeable, approachable guy. And he's very smart and incredibly charismatic—and knows it." He added that while Obama was "capable" of the intellectual exactitude required to win the presidency, he instead relied too heavily on his easy charm. "It's sort of like, 'That's all I need to get by,' which bespeaks sort of a condescending attitude towards the voters," the official told me. "And a laziness, an intellectual laziness."

He cited an example from *The Audacity of Hope* in which Obama complained that many "government programs don't work as advertised." Five days after the book was published in October 2006, Obama was asked to name some of those government programs by Tim Russert on NBC's *Meet the Press*. "And he can't give an example," the official told me. "Look, if you wrote the book, you should have thought through what it was. But he's sitting there, fumbling around." Obama did tell Russert that "we don't use electronic billing for Medicare and Medicaid providers." But the White House official pointed out to me that the vast majority of such transactions were indeed billed electronically. "He's lazy, so he hasn't figured that out," he told me. "And Russert of course is a journalist, so he's not obligated to."

The official ticked off several other examples. In March 2007, Obama was flummoxed by questions about his health care plan at a Democratic forum in Las Vegas. Two months later, the candidate drastically overstated the death toll from Kansas tornados. "Ten thousand people died," Obama told an audience, when the actual death toll was twelve.

"Over time," the White House official said, "we'll see other things like that. I'm going to be validated on Barack," he predicted. "He's not done the hard work necessary to prepare himself. And it's too late to do it."

But all this attention on Bush's potential successors obscured the fact that he still had more than a year left in his presidency. Granted, it was getting harder to enact his domestic agenda, as evidenced by his failure in late June 2007 to push through an immigration bill that would have granted legal status to illegal immigrants. Having already failed to reform Social Security in 2005, Bush now had little chance of enacting any major domestic initiatives during his remaining time in office. But he still had the power of the veto and enough support in Congress to sustain it. And so, legislatively, Bush switched from offense to defense.

While he could no longer aggressively enact a Republican agenda, he could certainly block enactment of a Democratic agenda, which was not an insignificant asset for a president nearing lame duck status. Moreover, Bush still wielded considerable constitutional powers that could be used in the event of a crisis or perhaps another vacancy on the Supreme Court. In the meantime, he didn't like talking about his legacy, preferring to let historians sort it out after he left office.

"I genuinely don't think he cares much about that, except in the grander view of when it's looked on twenty years from now. You know, will he have done the right thing in the major conflict of the day?" Bolten said. "His legacy will certainly be the first president to confront the war on terror. He won't win it. It's not like he will be Lincoln, who won the Civil War. And I think a lot of how history will judge his actions will depend on what happens between now and whenever the war on terror ends. And by the war on terror, I mean the war on Islamic extremism. People are a little gun-shy about saying it that way, but that's what's at the core. I think his legacy will be determined a lot by the course of that war over the next decade, two decades—who knows how long? I have conviction that he will be regarded as a truly courageous and—it's too big a word, *perspicacious*, he would never use that word—leader. And by perspicacious, I mean someone who saw the problem more clearly than others did—you know, as Churchill did of Hitler, or Roosevelt did—and helped lead the country in the right direction. So I think that will be the legacy."

Although Ken Mehlman didn't use the word *perspicacious*, he was similarly struck by the president's keen powers of understanding. Without prompting, the former Republican chief also invoked Churchill and Roosevelt when discussing Bush.

"First and foremost, he was someone who realistically saw the threat," Mehlman told me in his Washington law office. "If you stop and think about it, no nation that I can think of has ever preemptively addressed the threat—even when they should have. Churchill wasn't able to convince England to. FDR wasn't able to convince the United States to. And this president, while we were attacked, dealt with the threat. Did he deal with it imperfectly? Sure, as you do in every war. The Battle of the Bulge was unbelievably imperfect. Iwo Jima? Twice as many people died as died in Iraq. Lots of mistakes in tactics have been made. But what looms large? You don't remember Winston Churchill based on the specifics of how battles were fought. You remember that he stood, for a long time alone, and said this is a threat we have to deal with. He stood alone against the threat.

"This is a president who recognized the threat," Mehlman said of Bush. "He recognized that September 11 represented a fundamental pivot point in history, and had the moral clarity to see the nature of the threat, and to talk about what we need to do. That's huge."

Karl Rove said Bush would be remembered for the "moral realism" of his democracy agenda. "What American president in the foreseeable future is going to say, 'You know what? Let's not rock the boat. Let's accept the fact that we have authoritarian regimes that allow their people no means of expression, except through radical madrassas. We don't need to foster democracy,'" Rove told me. "It's going to be hard for any president of the United States to step away from the Bush Doctrine: if you feed a terrorist, arm a terrorist, train a terrorist, host a terrorist, you're just as bad as a terrorist. It's going to be very hard. People may be able to nibble around the edges, but future presidents—for the foreseeable future—are going to adopt the doctrine that we cannot wait until dangers fully materialize. We must take necessary preemptive action. The question is going to be what's necessary and preemptive, but that doctrine is ingrained."

Mehlman agreed. "I can't imagine even any Democrat—if a Democrat unfortunately is elected the next president—going back on the fundamental fact that there is this threat. Now, they may adopt the wrong tactics. But disagreements over whether you support the troops staying for another two years, or one year, in Iraq, is different from the paradigm shift. The paradigm shift was to say this is the twenty-first-century equivalent of war and it requires us to think differently about how we win those wars."

Still, the possibility of vindication by future historians wasn't much comfort to Bush in the midst of his seventh year as president. His popularity was being eroded by the daily tsunami of relentlessly negative news coverage, not to mention the increasingly bold attacks by left-lurching Democrats.

"This administration has been the worst in history," former president Jimmy Carter fulminated to the *Arkansas Democrat-Gazette* in May 2007. Truth be told, this particular criticism was so over the top that the White House considered it a political gift.

"That, frankly, is advantageous to us, because it reminds people that there are presidents like Jimmy Carter," a senior White House official told me. "Please, attack us every day."

There was a similar rally-around-the-president moment when Venezuelan dictator Hugo Chavez addressed the United Nations General Assembly one day after Bush.

"The devil came here yesterday," Chavez said from the same lectern Bush had used. "And it smells of sulfur still today."

And yet for every such buffoonish attack on Bush, there were countless other sober critiques that chipped away at his stature. In May 2007, a group of eleven moderate House Republicans came to the White House to warn Bush that his Iraq policy was rapidly losing support.

"It was a bunch of members coming in, saying, 'Mr. President, we want to support you, but our constituents are nowhere near where you are on the Iraq war—and neither are we,'" Bolten told me. "'We just have to tell you that you already have lost us, or you're on the verge of losing us, as a group of moderates.'"

By July, a number of Senate Republicans were also going wobbly, including Pete Domenici of New Mexico, Richard Lugar of Indiana, and George Voinovich of Ohio. This emboldened Democrats to renew their push for a withdrawal timetable.

Meanwhile, Scooter Libby was sentenced to thirty months in prison and fined $250,000, although Bush commuted his jail term. In Iraq, terrorists again bombed the Golden Mosque of Samarra, toppling a pair of ten-story minarets. This prompted another round of sectarian recriminations, although nothing approaching the sheer volume of violence that followed the first bombing.

All these developments took their toll on Bush's public standing. In the immediate aftermath of September 11, fully 90 percent of Americans had approved of the president's job performance—the highest level ever recorded by Gallup, which began taking such polls in 1938. But by July 2007, that number was down to 29 percent in a Gallup poll, Bush's lowest ever, having fallen thirteen points since December 2005 alone. (The Democratic Congress fared worse, with just 24 percent approval in the same survey.) Some polls by liberal news outlets showed approval ratings for Bush in the mid-twenties, which irritated a White House aide who regularly met with Bush in the Oval Office.

"Look, I'm a little bit of a hothead about it, so I'll walk in and get spun up about the latest stupid poll by CBS or the latest *New York Times* editorial," the aide told me. "And his attitude is a very healthy one. He says, 'Look, history will get it right and we'll both be dead. Who cares?' It's enormously liberating, and he's right. And look, I'm comfortable with what we're doing. And we don't need to sort of dismiss public opinion and public attitudes. But we do need to stay focused on what is right, in the country's interest, and divorce that from the current partisan environment."

To that end, Bush remained evangelical about the rightness of his presidency.

"I believe in the principles by which I have made decisions," he told me. "One principle is that the major role of the federal government in the beginning of the twenty-first century is to protect the American people from harm. And therefore my decisions have been all aimed at just doing that. Another principle is the universality of freedom. I firmly believe—and passionately believe—it's in this country's interest to challenge the status quo where there is resentment and hatred."

To implement this vision, Bush relied on a serenity that could come only from his evangelical faith in God. He told me he had "learned firsthand the power of faith to bring comfort in times of turbulence." He added: "The prayers of the American people have been influential on me because they have helped me sometimes achieve a sense of calm in the midst of the political storms."

Bush described his faith as a "walk" along a path that wound through both the public and private moments of his presidency. "My life is complex," he told me. "I don't think you can define a single moment that has defined my faith walk as a president. I think you have to look back at six and a half years and say it's the accumulation of a lot of powerful events."

Those ranged from the very public events of September 11 to the very private meetings Bush regularly held with the families of fallen soldiers. And there were plenty of other influences on the president's faith that were unknown to the public.

"The preachers at Camp David have been remarkable about affecting my faith," Bush said, citing one example. "So I mean, it's the sum effect of a series of remarkable experiences, some of which may seem to be meaningless on the surface—to others—but have a lot of meaning to me, that have affected my belief."

Those experiences would continue to shape Bush's faith as he contemplated the close of his presidency. He was already making plans for the Bush Institute, a think tank that would be attached to his presidential library, where he could continue promoting his democracy agenda. He also wanted to do some post-presidential work on his faith-based initiative, which allowed churches and other religious entities to help distribute federal assistance to the underprivileged.

"I'm thinking hard about that," Bush told me. "One of the great strengths of the country is the willingness of the average citizen to help a neighbor in need."

But Bush himself was also in need—of continuing spiritual guidance.

"I'm still a person seeking redemption," he told me. "I recognize that of all the people in the world, I need spiritual comfort and guidance and strength gained from prayer. But it's like life itself—life is a journey," he concluded. "It requires a lot of work and a lot of discipline and a lot of prayer. And therefore I view it as an incomplete journey—to be completed only upon death."

As the 2007 National Day of Prayer ceremony wound down, Bush returned to his seat in the East Room. He was pleased to see the benediction being delivered by an honest-to-God evangelical, a black Pentecostal bishop named Neavelle Coles.

"Lord, would you give wisdom to our leaders and courage to do what is right?" Coles prayed. "We know the race is not always to the fastest or the strongest, but to those who will endure."

When Coles finished, it was time for the closing song by the U.S. Army Chorus. The blue goose was removed from the riser so the dignitaries could have an unobstructed view of the singers. This time around, instead of taking center stage as a soloist, Sergeant Alvy Powell remained in the midst of his fellow soldiers. Their combined voices made a joyful noise as they launched into another African American spiritual, this one with a brisk tempo.

> *Soon we will be done with the troubles of the world*
> *The troubles of the world, the troubles of the world*
> *Soon we will be done with the troubles of the world*
> *Goin' home to live with God . . .*

They repeated the chorus, lowering their voices with each line, until they sounded like monks murmuring in a monastery. And then, just when the audience was being lulled into a reverie, the decibel level exploded as the soldiers launched into the first verse.

> *I WANT (I want!) to meet my mother*
> *I WANT (I want!) to meet my mother*
> *I WANT (I want!) to meet my mother*
> *I'm goin' to live with God!*

Bush moved his head with the music, which by now had everyone's undivided attention. There was another round of monk-like murmuring, followed by an even more startling explosion of manful voices.

> *No more (no more!) weepin' and a-wailin' (wailin'!)*
> *No more (no more!) weepin' and a-wailin' (wailin'!)*
> *No more (no more!) weepin' and a-wailin'*
> *I'm goin' to live with God!*

The forcefulness of the sound was downright exhilarating. One could almost envision meeting one's Maker. The evangelical president wiped the edges of his eyes.

I WANT (I want!) to meet my Jesus
I WANT (I want!) to meet my Jesus
I WANT (I want!) to meet my Jesus
I'm goin' to live with God!
I'm goin' to live with GOD!
I'm goin' to LIVE WITH GOD!

ACKNOWLEDGMENTS

Coming down the home stretch of a manuscript is the time when having a spouse like Becky makes all the difference. She cheerfully accepted my utter abdication of household chores, parental duties, and various other responsibilities, such as shaving. So did our children, Brittany, Brooke, Ben, Billy, and Blair. So I must thank my family, first and foremost, for hanging in there while I completed *The Evangelical President*.

Professionally speaking, this book could not have been written without the unwavering support of Vivienne Sosnowski, national editorial director of Clarity Media Group. Equally steadfast were my colleagues at Clarity's flagship paper, the *Washington Examiner*, including publisher Michael Phelps, executive editor Steve Smith, and national security correspondent Rowan Scarborough.

It's a privilege to write a book for professionals like Tom Phillips and Jeff Carneal, chairman and president, respectively, of Eagle Publishing. Ditto for Marji Ross, president of Eagle's subsidiary, Regnery

Publishing. I owe Regnery executive editor Harry Crocker a debt of gratitude for coming up with the title and, in large part, the concept for this book. And editor Tim Carney made many improvements to the manuscript.

A special word of thanks goes to Roger Ailes, Brit Hume, and all my many friends at FOX News Channel.

Finally, I'm indebted to President Bush, Vice President Cheney, Karl Rove, Josh Bolten, and all the other sources, both inside and outside the administration, who helped me make sense of these momentous times.

INDEX

A

ABC, 33, 68, 77, 79, 123, 135, 150, 186

abortion: Bush, George W. and, 25, 176–80, 183; Catholicism and, 181–82; Clinton, Bill and, 177; Constitution, U.S. and, 173, 179, 182; *Doe v. Bolton* and, 177; effects of, 180; mother's health and, 177, 182; partial-birth, 173–83; rights of unborn and, 178–79; *Roe v. Wade* and, 173, 182, 183; Supreme Court, U.S. and, 173–83; women's health and, 177, 179, 181

Abu Ghraib prison, Iraq, 55, 60, 107

Acts of the Apostles, 14, 18

Affleck, Ben, 4–5, 9

Afghanistan, 47–48, 161

Africa, 25, 27

AIDS, 25

Air Force One, 109

al-Arabiya, 92

alcohol, 17, 18–19

Alito, Samuel, 173, 174, 180, 182

Allah, 164

Allen, George, 158; 2006 midterm elections and, 153–54, 158; "macaca" scandal of, 11, 115–21, 137; presidential prospects of, 121–22, 137–38, 153

Allen, Jennifer, 120

al Qaeda, 11, 40, 166; ideology of, 108; sectarian violence in Iraq and, 113; al-Zarqawi, Abu Musab, death of and, 108

America: messianic tradition of, 28; religion in, 9
American Theocracy (Phillips), 5–6
Amin, Rizgar Muhammad, 57
Anbar province, Iraq, 33–34, 95–96, 165
Andover, Mass., 16
AP. *See* Associated Press
apocalypse, 6–7, 18
Arkansas Democrat-Gazette, 213
Armageddon, 6–7
Armitage, Richard, 141–42
Armstrong, Katharine, 65–67, 69, 72
Armstrong Ranch, Texas, 64
Associated Press (AP), 67, 123
The Audacity of Hope (Obama), 207, 210
Axelrod, Jim, 72, 74, 77, 78, 83
Ayoub, Bashar Mahmoud, 35

B

Baath Party, 53, 168
Backus, Jenny, 76
Badri, Haitham al-, 92
Bahjat, Atwar, 92–93
Balkin, Jack M., 181
Bartlett, Dan, 82
Bayh, Evan, 125
BBC, 56
Beran, Michael Knox, 28
Berg, Nick, 91
Berger, Sandy, 142–45
Bible, 7, 18, 154
Biden, Joe, 119; botched jokes and, 118; Bush, George W., use of prayer by and, 3–4; creationism and, 8–9; evangelical Christians and, 4

bin Laden, Osama, 52, 91, 105, 161; September 11 and, 90; al-Zarqawi, Abu Musab and, 91, 92
Blair, Tony, 107
Blitzer, Wolf, 148–49
Bolten, Josh, 97, 113, 185, 202–3; 2006 midterm elections and, 158; Bush, George W., faith of and, 28; Bush, George W., legacy of and, 211–12; Bush, George W., tolerance of and, 24; Election 2008 and, 206; Iraq and, 190–91, 214; Rumsfeld, Donald, resignation of and, 159–60; spending and, 155–56
Borger, Gloria, 78
Broder, David, 142, 189
Brokeback Mountain, 75
Brown, Campbell, 39
Burr, Aaron, 74
Bush, George H. W., 9, 16, 17, 133, 195; faith of, 29–30; Hussein, Saddam and, 61
Bush, George W.: 2006 midterm elections and, 128–29, 131, 154, 157; abortion and, 25, 176–80, 183; alcohol and, 17, 18–19; Cheney, Dick hunting accident and, 65, 74, 75, 78; conservatism and, 2, 27, 141; conversion of, 19–20, 29; education and, 16, 25, 26; Election 2008 and, 201–8; as evangelical Christian, 4, 9–11, 19–20; faith of, 1–11, 15–20, 215–16; as "Freevangelical," 28–29; Hurricane Katrina and, 46; Iraq policy of, 30, 96–97, 112–13, 130–33, 158–62, 166–71, 186; Iraq visit of, 109–10; Iraq

war and, 1–3, 9–10, 25–26, 36, 37, 48–49; job approval ratings of, 39–40; judicial nominations of, 173, 177; legacy of, 211–13; media leaks and, 145–46; Memogate and, 139–41; missile defense and, 64; "Mission Accomplished" speech of, 107; National Day of Prayer (2007) and, 197–200, 216–18; Nixon, Richard and, 37; PATRIOT Act and, 193; prayer and, 1–4, 17, 19–20, 21–22, 197–200; public piety of, 23, 26, 147; public policy and, 24–27, 178; September 11 and, 10, 21–23, 29, 41, 168, 212; spending and, 155–56; stem cell research and, 24; terrorist surveillance program and, 100; as true believer, 29–30; vision of, 9–11; war on terrorism and, 9, 27, 211; welfare and, 25; al-Zarqawi, Abu Musab, death of and, 106

Bush Institute, 216

Bush, Laura, 13, 17, 31, 98, 101; Bush, George W., drinking of and, 18; tolerance of, 24

C

Cafferty, Jack, 83

California, partial-birth abortion in, 179

Camp David, 101–3, 216

Card, Andy, 97; Cheney, Dick hunting accident and, 65, 88; Kerry, John botched joke and, 137

Carter, Jimmy, 5, 30, 213

cartoon intifada, 104

Casey, George, 93

Catholicism, Catholic Church, abortion and, 181–82

CBS, 39, 68, 72, 73, 75, 77, 78, 83, 86, 88, 123, 139–40, 150, 215

CBS *Evening News*, 73, 83, 140

Central Intelligence Agency (CIA), 41, 44, 46, 145, 147, 203

A Charge to Keep (Bush), 14, 16, 17, 18

Chavez, Hugo, 213–14

Cheney, Dick, 109, 142, 165, 185; 2006 midterm elections and, 133, 154–55, 156–57; in Afghanistan, 47–48; Bush, George W., faith of and, 26–27; Democratic attacks on, 10–11; Election 2008 and, 206; health of, 192; hunting accident of, 11, 63–88; Iraq and, 36–37, 40, 185–87, 188; Iraq visit of, 33–37; Kerry, John botched joke and, 136; Lieberman, Joe and, 126–28, 156–57; mainstream media and, 194; media leaks and, 146–47; as most powerful vice president in history, 78, 194–95; PATRIOT Act and, 42–43; Plame affair and, 46; secret prisons and, 43–44; sectarian violence in Iraq and, 94, 95; September 11 and, 36; torturing of terrorism suspects and, 41–42; war on terrorism and, 36–37, 49–50, 126–27, 193–94

Cheney, Dick hunting accident: Armstrong, Katharine and, 66, 67, 69, 72; Bush, George W. and, 65, 74, 75, 78; Card, Andy and, 65, 88; Clinton, Hillary Rodham and, 79–80;

Cheney, Dick hunting accident
(continued): Gregory, David
and, 69–72, 73, 76, 77–78,
83–86; Hume, Brit and, 80–83;
Hurricane Katrina and, 73, 78;
late-night comics and, 75–76;
mainstream media and, 64, 66,
68–75, 76–79, 80, 81–88;
McClellan, Scott and, 65,
68–73, 75, 76–78, 85; political
fallout of, 67; Rove, Karl and,
65, 83, 85; Schieffer, Bob and,
73–74, 78; White House press
corps and, 68–75, 76–79, 80, 82,
83, 85–86, 88; Whittington,
Harry and, 62–67, 69, 71, 72, 77,
79, 80, 81, 83–85
Cheney, Lynne, 148–49
Chicago Tribune, 181
Chicago, University of, 181
Christian Coalition of America, 27
Christianity. *See* faith; religion
"Church of the Presidents." *See* St.
John's Episcopal Church, Wash-
ington, D.C.
Churchill, Winston, 212
CIA. *See* Central Intelligence
Agency
Civil War, U.S., 27–28, 211
Clark, Ramsey, 56–58
Clinton, Bill, 23, 29, 74, 79, 125, 135,
191; abortion, partial-birth and,
177; Iraq, withdrawal of troops
from and, 187–88; terrorism
and, 142–45
Clinton, Hillary Rodham: botched
jokes and, 118, 119; Cheney,
Dick hunting accident and,
79–80; Election 2008 and,
201–2, 208–10; Iraq and, 110–11,

203–5; Kerry, John botched joke
and, 136; presidential prospects
of, 200–201
Clooney, George, 139
CNN, 83, 86, 125, 148, 158
Cold War, 126, 202
Coles, Neavelle, 216
Communism, 126
conservatism, conservatives: Bush,
George W. and, 2, 141; compas-
sionate, 27; fiscal, 155–56; racism
and, 118–19; reform and, 156
Constitution, U.S.: abortion and,
173, 179, 182; PATRIOT Act
and, 43; terrorist surveillance
program and, 100
Contract With America, 156
Cook, Charlie, 121
Cooper, Matt, 68
Corpus Christi Caller-Times, 67, 82,
87, 88
Cottle, Michelle, 21
Countdown, 76
Cox Newspapers, 96, 130
creationism, 7–9
Crowley, Candy, 86
Cunningham, Randy "Duke," 122

D

Darfur, Sudan, 25, 26, 27
Dawa Party, 54, 55
Dean, Howard, 37, 42–43
Deans, Bob, 96
Declaration of Independence, 179
DeLay, Tom, 121
democracy: in Afghanistan, 47–48;
in Iraq, 34, 35, 37, 108, 127; in
Middle East, 29
Democratic Party, Democrats:
2006 midterm elections and,

121, 154–55, 157–61; botched jokes and, 118–19; Bush, George W. as "decider" and, 97–98; Bush, George W., attacks on by, 10–11; Hussein, Saddam, trial of and, 52; Iraq and, 96, 111, 129–30, 168, 187–92; Lieberman, Joe and, 38, 124–26; PATRIOT Act and, 42–43, 193; religion and, 4; Rumsfeld, Donald and, 108; scandals of, 124; terrorist surveillance program and, 100; war on terrorism and, 127, 192–94

Denmark, 101, 103–4

Department of Justice, U.S. (DOJ), 144

Dodd, Chris, 125

Doe v. Bolton, 177

DOJ. *See* Department of Justice, U.S.

Domenici, Pete, 214

domestic spying, 40

Drudge Report, 67, 150

Dujail massacre, 52–55, 56, 164, 165

E

Earle, Ronnie, 122

Early Show, 68, 75

education: Bush, George W. and, 25, 26; injustice and, 26; "no child left behind" and, 16

Edwards, John, 203

Egypt, 14, 49

Eisenhower, Dwight, 30, 102, 103, 202

Election 2006: Allen, George and, 153–54, 158; Bolten, Josh and, 158; Bush, George W. and, 128–29, 131, 154, 157–61; Cheney,

Dick and, 133, 154–55, 156; Democratic Party and, 154–55, 157; Iraq and, 158–61; Kerry, John botched joke and, 133–37; Lieberman, Joe and, 156, 156–57; Republican Party and, 121–24, 154–56; Rove, Karl and, 156; spending and, 155–56

Election 2008: Bolten, Josh and, 206; Bush, George W. and, 201–8; Cheney, Dick and, 206; Clinton, Hillary Rodham and, 201–2, 208–10; Iraq and, 201–7; Obama, Barack and, 210–11; Rove, Karl and, 201

Emancipation Proclamation, 198

Epstein, Joseph, 29–30

Europe, secret prisons in, 43–44, 147

evangelical Christians: Biden, Joe and, 4; Bush, George W. and, 4, 9–11, 19–20; conversion experience and, 19; creationism and, 9; media attacks on, 23; proselytizing and, 24

Evans, Don, 18

evolution, 7–9

F

faith: importance of, 22; public policy and, 24–27, 178; science and, 5; serenity and, 28. *See also* religion

Feingold, Russ, 100, 125

Fighting Back (Sammon), 10

Fitzgerald, Patrick, 141

Foley, Laurence, 91

Foley, Mark, 122–23

Ford, Gerald, 195

Ford, Harold, 136

FOX News, 27, 80, 83, 106, 220
Frank, Barney, 123
Freevangelicals, 28–29
fundamentalism: Christian, 5; Islamic, 5; public policy and religious, 180

G
Gandhi, Mahatma, 118
Garcia, Kathryn, 67
Gates, Robert, 133, 159
Gibson, Charlie, 68, 135
God: belief in, 2; war on terrorism and, 200. *See also* faith; religion
Golden Mosque, Samarra, Iraq, 89–90, 92–93, 113, 166, 186
Goldwater, Barry, 156
Golf Cart One, 102
Gonzales, Alberto, 192
Good Morning America, 68, 79, 150
Good Night, and Good Luck, 139
GOP. *See* Republican Party, Republicans
Gore, Al, 83, 195
Graham, Billy, 17, 19
Greece, 14
Green, John, 23–24, 150
Greenhouse, Linda, 180–81, 183
Gregory, David, Cheney, Dick hunting accident and, 69–72, 73, 76, 77–78, 83–86
Guantanamo Bay, Cuba, 202

H
Hadley, Stephen, 106
Haideri, Ali Hassan al-, 60, 61
Hakimiyah prison, Iraq, 55, 60
Hamas, 86
Hamilton, Alexander, 74

Hardball with Chris Matthews, 79, 121
Hart, Melissa, 128
Harvard Business School, 16
Haskell, Martin, 174–75
Hastert, Denny, 122
health care, 210
Hennen, Scott, 42, 147
Herman, Ken, 130
Hewitt, Hugh, 33
Heyward, Andrew, 140
Hezbollah, 131
Hitler, Adolf, 212
Hollywood, 1, 9, 117
Hostettler, John, 128
House Committee on Oversight and Government Reform, 145
Houston, Tex., 15–16
Howard, Josh, 140
Howell, Deborah, 87
Hume, Brit, 27; Cheney, Dick hunting accident and, 80–83
Hurricane Katrina, 46, 73, 78
Hussein, King, 91
Hussein, Qusay, 185
Hussein, Saddam, 35, 37, 42–43, 95, 99, 168, 185, 206; Bush, George W. and, 51–52, 55–56, 61–62; capture of, 56, 186; Dujail massacre and, 52–55, 56, 164; execution of, 163–65, 186; Iran and, 52; Iraq war and, 39; trial of, 11, 51–52, 56–61, 113; WMD and, 36
Hussein, Uday, 185

I
Imus, Don, 135
Independents (in Congress), 154
International Criminal Court, 57

International Red Cross, 44

Iran, 14, 54, 167, 168; Hussein, Saddam and, 52; nuclear program of, 64, 78

Iraq, 14; 2006 midterm elections and, 158–61; Bush, George W. and, 158–62; Bush, George W. visit to, 109–10; Cheney, Dick visit to, 33–37; Clinton, Hillary Rodham and, 203–5; democracy in, 34, 35, 37, 108, 127; Democratic Party, Democrats and, 168, 187–92; Election 2008 and, 201–7; evolving policy in, 158–62, 166–71, 186–87; Golden Mosque, Samarra bombing in, 89–90, 92–93; nuclear program of, 168; Obama, Barack and, 203; presidential politics and, 191–92; progress in, 38–39; sectarian violence in, 90–91, 92, 93–96, 113, 124, 166–67, 169, 186; successes in, 185–86; Sunni insurgency in, 33, 34, 166, 186; withdrawal of troops from, 96, 110–12, 187–91. *See also* Iraq war

Iraq Study Group, 166

Iraq war: apocalypse and, 6–7; beginning of, 2; Bush, George W. and, 1–3, 9–10, 25–26, 30, 36, 37, 48–49; Cheney, Dick and, 36–37; Denmark and, 103–4; Hussein, Saddam and, 39; mainstream media and, 38–40, 49, 124, 150; moral ramifications of, 26; public support for, 130–31, 159; Rumsfeld, Donald and, 2; torturing of terrorism suspects and, 41–42. *See also* Iraq

Iraqi Special Tribunal, 57–58

Islamic fundamentalism, 5

Israel, 131

J

Jaafari, Ibrahim al-, 96

Jefferson, Thomas, 20

Jefferson, William, 124

Jesus Christ, 14, 18, 20, 25, 29

Johnson, Lyndon, 30, 56

Joint Chiefs of Staff, 166

Jordan, 91, 96, 186

K

Kabul, Afghanistan, 47

Keller, Bill, 23, 26, 147, 148

Kennedy, Anthony, 174, 180–81

Kennedy, John F., 30, 126

Kerry, John, 123, 125, 142, 209–10; botched joke of, 133–37; Iraq, withdrawal of troops from and, 110, 111–12

Khalilzad, Zalmay, 96, 106

Kharzai, Hamid, 47–48

Koran, 60

Kurtz, Howard, 86–87

L

LaHood, Ray, 106

Lamont, Ned, 125, 126, 156

Laster, John, 144

Lauer, Matt, 137

Lawn, Connie, 72

Leach, Jim, 128

Lebanon, 104, 131, 170

Leno, Jay, 140

León, Reverend Dr. Luis, 14, 30–31

Letterman, David, 75

Levin, Carl, 112

Libby, Lewis "Scooter," 46, 142, 214

Lieberman, Joe, 207; 2006
    midterm elections and, 154,
    156; Bush, George W., defense
    of by, 37–38, 124–25; Cheney,
    Dick defense of, 38, 126–28;
    Democratic ostracizing of, 38,
    124–26; Independent Party
    and, 154, 156; mainstream
    media and, 125

Limbaugh, Rush, 200–201

Lincoln, Abraham, 20, 27–28, 30,
    198–99, 211

Lockhart, Joe, 80

Los Angeles Times, 56, 87, 149

Lugar, Richard, 214

Lynch, Rick, 95

M

McCarthy, Joseph, 139

McCarthy, Terry, 186

McClellan, Scott, 97; Cheney,
    Dick hunting accident and, 65,
    68–73, 75, 76–78, 82, 85

McGovern, George, 191

McKinney, Cynthia, 124

Madison, James, 14

Maer, Peter, 73

Maher, Bill, 14, 200; Bush, George
    W., faith of and, 1–9

mainstream media: anti-military
    bias of, 33, 149–50; botched
    jokes and, 118–19; Bush, George
    W., faith of and, 20–21, 23–24;
    Cheney, Dick hunting accident
    and, 64, 66, 68–75, 76–79, 80,
    81–88; "domestic spying" and,
    40; double standard of, 121, 123,
    142; evangelical Christians and,

23; Hurricane Katrina and, 46;
    Hussein, Saddam, execution of
    and, 165; Hussein, Saddam, trial
    of and, 52, 61; Iraq war and,
    38–40, 49, 124, 150; Kerry, John
    botched joke and, 134–35, 137;
    leaking of information by,
    43–44, 145–48; liberal bias of,
    121, 150–51; Lieberman, Joe and,
    125; Plame affair and, 46, 141;
    Republican scandals and,
    121–24; war on terrorism and,
    148–49

Maliki, Nouri al-, 96, 109–10, 113;
    sectarian violence in Iraq and,
    167; al-Zarqawi, Abu Musab,
    death of and, 106–7

Mapes, Mary, 139

Marine One, 109

Matalin, Mary, 87–88

Matthews, Chris, 79

media. *See* mainstream media

Media Research Center, 83, 123

Medicaid, 27, 210

Medicare, 27, 210

Meet the Press, 85, 210

Mehlman, Ken, 128, 212, 213; Bush,
    George W., faith of and, 26;
    Iraq and, 189–90; spending and,
    156

Memogate, 139–41

Midland, Tex., 16–17

Miers, Harriet, 192

Milbank, Dana, 75–76, 87

Miss Beazley, 13, 14, 31

missile defense, 64

Misunderestimated (Sammon), 10

Mohammed, Ahmed Hassan,
    58–60

Mohammed, Khalid Sheikh, 44
Montopoli, Brian, 150
Moonves, Leslie, 140
Moran, Terry, 38, 149, 165; Cheney, Dick interview with, 33–37, 40–47; Hurricane Katrina and, 46; PATRIOT Act and, 42–43; Plame affair and, 46; secret prisons and, 43–44; torturing of terrorism suspects and, 41–42
MoveOn.org, 38, 99, 100
MSNBC, 75–76, 79, 118, 121
Mubarak, Hosni, 49
Muhammad, Prophet, 104, 164
mujahideen, 161–62
Murphy, Mary, 140
Murrow, Edward R., 139
Myers, Dee Dee, 79

N
National Archives document theft, 142–45
National Day of Prayer (2007), 197–200, 216–18
National Review, 28
National Security Council, 166
NBC, 69, 73, 77, 80, 83, 85, 87, 123, 137, 210
NBC News, 39
NBC *Nightly News*, 73, 83
Nebraska, partial-birth abortion in, 179
New Republic magazine, 21
New York, partial-birth abortion in, 179
New York Daily News, 68
New York Times, 23, 38, 40, 57, 61, 68, 75, 76, 79, 82, 83, 88, 97, 112, 135, 145, 146–47, 180, 181, 183, 186, 192, 193, 202, 215
Newsweek, 6, 86, 91, 141, 142
Newton, Isaac, 5
Nightline, 33
9-11 Commission, 40–41, 142–43, 146
Nixon, Richard, 5, 30, 37, 195
North Korea, 64
Nuaimi, Najeeb al-, 58

O
Obama, Barack, 191; Bush, George W., criticism of by, 207–8; Election 2008 and, 210–11; health care and, 210; Iraq and, 203–5; lack of preparedness of, 210–11
O'Connor, Sandra Day, 173, 179
Olbermann, Keith, 76, 79
Operation Iraqi Freedom. *See* Iraq war
Operation Together Forward, 113, 166

P
Pakistan, 49
partial-birth abortion: ban on, 173–83; Bush, George W. and, 176–80, 183; Catholicism and, 181–82; Constitution, U.S. and, 173, 179; effects of, 180; reality of, 174–75; mother's health and, 182; Supreme Court, U.S. and, 173–75; women's health and, 181
Partial-Birth Abortion Ban Act, 175
PATRIOT Act, 42–43, 127, 193
Pelosi, Nancy, 125, 133, 157–58, 189, 190

Peloton One, 102
Pentecost, 14, 18
Petraeus, David, 185–87, 201, 206
Phillips, Kevin, 5–7, 14
Phillips Academy, 16
Pizzey, Allen, 150–51
Plame, Valerie, 46
Plame affair: Cheney, Dick and, 46; mainstream media and, 46, 141; Rove, Karl and, 141–42
Plante, Bill, 75, 86–87
Pope, Alexander, 5
Powell, Alvy, 197–98, 217
Powell, Colin, 141
Prairie Chapel Ranch, 102
prayer: Bush, George W. and, 1–4, 19–20, 21–22, 197–200; effectiveness of, 1; importance of, 19–20; National Day of Prayer (2007) and, 197–200; rejection of, 17; Republican Party and, 3
prisons, secret, 43–44, 147
Psalms, 198–99
public policy: faith and, 24–27, 178; religious fundamentalism and, 180

Q
Qassem, Abdul Karim, 53
Quayle, Dan, 195

R
Raddatz, Martha, 77
Rahman, Sheikh Abd al-, 104
Ramadan, Taha Yasin, 55
Rasmussen, Anders Fogh, 101–2, 103–4, 108–9
Rasmussen Reports, 88
Rather, Dan, 139, 140–41

Reagan, Ronald, 28, 30, 98, 156
Real Time, 1, 4
Reed, Jack, 112
Reed, Ralph, 27
Reid, Harry, 124, 125; Iraq and, 188–89, 191, 206; Lieberman, Joe and, 38; PATRIOT Act and, 42–43, 127, 193
Reliable Sources, 86
religion: in America, 9; Democratic Party, Democrats and, 4; political, 29; politics and, 5, 24; Republicans and, 5. *See also* faith
Republican National Committee (RNC), 26, 128
Republican Party, Republicans, 212; 2006 midterm elections and, 11, 121–22, 154–56; prayer and, 3; alleged racism of, 118–19; religion and, 5; scandals of, 121–24; spending and, 155–56; taxation and, 157; Vietnam War and, 37; Watergate and, 37
Revelation, 6–7
RNC. *See* Republican National Committee
Roberts, John, 173, 174, 182
Roe v. Wade, 173, 182, 183
rogue regimes, 64, 168
Rome, Italy, 14
Roosevelt, Franklin D., 28, 45–46, 103, 212
Rove, Karl, 97, 128, 192; 2006 midterm elections and, 156; Bush, George W., faith of and, 22–23, 25; Bush, George W., legacy of and, 212–13; Cheney,

Dick hunting accident and, 65, 83, 85; Election 2008 and, 201; Plame affair and, 141–42

Rumsfeld, Donald, 38, 97, 136; Bush, George W. Iraq policy and, 131–33; Democratic Party, Democrats and, 108; Iraq war and, 2; resignation of, 131–33, 159–60; al-Zarqawi, Abu Musab, death of and, 106, 108

Russert, Tim, 80, 85, 210

Ruwaid, Abdullah Kadam al-, 55

Ruwaid, Misher Abdullah, 55

S

Sadr, Moqtada al-, 163

Sadr, Muhammad Baqir al-, 163

Salinas, Ramon, III, 65–66

Sanders, Bernie, 154

Sanger, David, 75, 76

San Miguel, Gilberto, Jr., 66–67

Saudi Arabia, 14, 49, 96

Scalia, Antonin, 174, 182

Schieffer, Bob, 39, 73–74, 78

Schumer, Charles, 125, 188

September 11, 31–32, 39–40; bin Laden, Osama and, 90; Bush, George W. and, 10, 21–23, 29, 41, 168, 212; Cheney, Dick and, 36; significance of, 212; war on terrorism and, 10

Shakespeare, William, 5

Sherwood, Don, 122

Shipman, Claire, 80

Sidarth, S. R., 115–18, 119

Siegel, Michael, 198–99

Siegel, Reva B., 181

Simpson, Alan, 74–75, 88

60 Minutes, 140

60 Minutes II, 140

Snow, Tony, 97, 146, 147–48

Social Security, 99, 211

Special Report (FOX News Channel), 83

Stein, Joel, 149–50

stem cell research, 24

Stephanopoulos, George, 74, 135

St. John's Episcopal Church, Washington, D.C., 13–15, 30–31

Stone, Geoffrey R., 181–82

Strategery (Sammon), 10

Studds, Gerry, 123

Sudan, 25

Supreme Court, U.S.: abortion, partial-birth and, 173–83; Bush, George W. nominations to, 173, 177

Syria, 96, 104, 168

T

taxation, 157

Taylor, Harry, 99–100

terrorism: apocalypse and, 6–7; financial tracking of, 145–46; state sponsors of, 36–37; surveillance program and, 100, 147, 192–93; torturing of suspects and, 41–42

Texas, University of, 76

Thomas, Clarence, 174, 182

Thomas, Helen, 135

Tikriti, Barzan al-: Dujail massacre and, 54–55, 165; execution of, 165; trial of, 58–60

Time magazine, 68

Today show, 80, 87, 137

Tonight Show, 140

Treasury Department, U.S., 145

Truman, Harry S., 28, 30, 202
Turkey, 14

U
UAE. *See* United Arab Emirates
UN. *See* United Nations
United Arab Emirates (UAE), 98
United Nations (UN), 57
USA Radio Network, 72

V
Vargas, Elizabeth, 38–39
Vatican, 181
Vieira del Mello, Sérgio, 91
Vietnam War, 37, 68
Virginia Tech massacre (2007), 199
Voinovich, George, 214

W
Warner, John, 153
war on terrorism: Bush, George W.
   and, 9, 27, 211; Cheney, Dick
   and, 36–37, 49–50, 126–27,
   193–94; as "crusade," 26; Democratic Party and, 127, 192–94;
   mainstream media and, 148–49;
   PATRIOT Act and, 193;
   progress in, 49–50; September
   11 and, 10; terrorist surveillance
   program and, 192–93
Washington, George, 199
Washington Post, 23, 41, 43, 68, 75,
   76, 79, 87, 88, 118, 119, 120, 121,
   135, 142, 145, 147, 188, 189

Watergate, 37
weapons of mass destruction
   (WMD), 36
Webb, James, 115, 116, 119, 153–54
Weekly Standard, 29
Weldon, Curt, 122
welfare, 25
West, Betsy, 140
Whittington, Harry, Cheney,
   Dick hunting accident and,
   62–67, 69, 71, 72, 77, 79, 80, 81,
   83–85
Whittington, Merce, 83
Wilson, Joseph, 141
WMD. *See* weapons of mass
   destruction
World News Tonight, 77
World War II, 45–46

Y
Yale Law School, 181
Yale University, 7, 16
Yellin, Jessica, 68
YouTube, 119
Yu, Eun-Jae, 199

Z
Zarqawi, Abu Musab al-, 11, 52, 131,
   185–86; bin Laden, Osama and,
   91, 92; death of, 104–8, 112–13,
   186; Golden Mosque, Samarra
   bombing and, 90–91; sectarian
   violence and, 93–96
Zawahiri, Ayman al-, 161–62